A FINE & PRIVATE PLACE

**Book and Lyrics by
ERIK HAAGENSEN**

**Music by
RICHARD ISEN**

SAMUEL FRENCH, INC.

45 WEST 25TH STREET   NEW YORK 10010
7623 SUNSET BOULEVARD   HOLLYWOOD 90046
LONDON   *TORONTO*

Copyright © 1989, 1992 by Erik Haagensen and Richard Isen

Amateurs wishing to arrange for the production of A FINE AND PRIVATE PLACE must make application to SAMUEL FRENCH, INC., at 45 West 25th Street, New York, NY 10010, giving the following particulars:

(1) The name of the town and theatre or hall of the proposed production.

(2) The maximum seating capacity of the theatre or hall.

(3) Scale of ticket prices.

(4) The number of performances intended and the dates thereof.

(5) Indicate whether you will use an orchestration or simply a piano.

Upon receipt of these particulars SAMUEL FRENCH, INC., will quote terms and availability.

Stock royalty quoted on application to SAMUEL FRENCH, INC., 45 West 25th Street, New York, NY 10010.

For all other rights than those stipulated above, apply to Harold Messing, Esq., 433 N. Camden Drive, Suite 1111, Beverly Hills, CA 90210

An orchestration consisting of:

Piano/conductor's score

Bass

Percussion

will be loaned two months prior to the production ONLY on receipt of the royalty quoted for all performances, the rental fee and a refundable deposit. The deposit will be refunded on the safe return to SAMUEL FRENCH, INC. of all materials loaned for the production.

Printed in the U.S.A.
ISBN 0 573 69353 6

IMPORTANT BILLING AND CREDIT REQUIREMENTS

All producers of A FINE AND PRIVATE PLACE *must* give credit to the Authors of the Work in all programs distributed in connection with performances of the Work, and in all instances in which the title of the Work appears for the purposes of advertising, publicizing or otherwise exploiting a production thereof; including, without limitation to, programs, souvenir books and playbills. The names of the Authors *must* also appear on a separate line in which no other matter appears, immediately following the title of the Work, and *must* be in size of type not less than 75% of the size of type of the largest letter used in the title of the Work. Billing *must* be substantially as follows:

(Name of Producer)
presents

A FINE AND PRIVATE PLACE

Book and Lyrics by   Music by
ERIK HAAGENSEN   RICHARD ISEN

Based upon the book by Peter S. Beagle

Musical Arrangements by Henry Aronson

Wherever the dramatists receive credit, directly beneath the credit to the dramatists and in type and prominence at least 50% of the type and prominence of the names of the dramatists the credit "based upon the book by Peter S. Beagle" must appear.

The following credits *must* also appear in all programs:

"A Fine and Private Place" was partially developed and received staged readings at the O'Neill Theatre Center's 1987 National Music Theatre Conference."

"Originally produced by Goodspeed Opera House, Michael P. Price, Executive Producer."

GOODSPEED OPERA HOUSE

at

THE NORMA TERRIS THEATRE

MICHAEL P. PRICE
Executive Producer

DAN SIRETTA
Associate Artistic Director

LYNN CRIGLER
Musical Director

SUE FROST
Associate Producer

WARREN PINCUS
Casting Director

presents

A new musical-in-progress
based on the novel by
Peter S. Beagle

Book and Lyrics by
ERIK HAAGENSEN

Music by
RICHARD ISEN

Scenery and Lighting by
FRED KOLO

Technical Director
JOHN HUGH MINOR

Stage Manager
RUTH M. FELDMAN

Musical Direction by
HENRY ARONSON

Directed by
ROBERT KALFIN

Presented by arrangement with Steven H. David.

_______________________ August 3 through August 20, 1989 _______________________

CAST OF CHARACTERS
(In order of appearance)

Jonathan Rebeck .... Charles Goff

Raven .... Gabriel Barre

Michael Morgan .... Brian Sutherland

Gertrude Klapper .... Evalyn Baron

Laura Durand .... Maureen Silliman

Campos .... Larri Rebbega

MUSICIANS

Keyboard .... Henry Aronson

Percussion .... Sal Ranniello

MUSICAL NUMBERS

Act I

Act II

CHARACTERS

JONATHAN REBECK—Mid-50's. Smallish. Unassuming. Philosophical. Precise. *High baritone.*

GERTRUDE KLAPPER—Early 60's. Talkative. Vital. Unceremonious. Jewish. *Alto.*

MICHAEL MORGAN—A ghost. Mid-30's. Preppy. Witty. Defensive. Smooth. *Tenor.*

LAURA DURAND—Another ghost. Mid-30's. Plain. Smart. Inexperienced. Romantic. *Soprano.*

THE RAVEN—Cynical. Selfish. Omniscient. Feathered. *Non-singing.*

CAMPOS—25-45. Cuban. Earthy. Fatalistic. Lubricated. *Non-singing.*

(THE RAVEN and CAMPOS are to be played by the same actor.)

PLACE
Yorkchester Cemetery, a vernal oasis in the Bronx.

TIME
Early summer. This year.

"The grave's a fine and private place,
But none, I think, do there embrace."

—Andrew Marvell,
"To His Coy Mistress"

[Music Cue #1: OPENING]

PROLOGUE

The LIGHTS come up on Yorkchester Cemetery, a pastoral oasis in the middle of the Bronx. The stage picture is an inviting, stylized rendering of greenery, trees, winding roads, and buildings that have the shape of houses. JONATHAN REBECK sits on the steps of a mausoleum, absorbed in a chess problem. Suddenly, with a whoosh, something flies over the heads of the audience. A baloney falls from the sky and scatters the chessboard and pieces. The RAVEN appears and perches on a corner of Rebeck's mausoleum.

REBECK. *(After a beat, looking up.)* A whole baloney! How did you manage to lift it?
RAVEN. Damn near ruptured myself.
REBECK. *(Gathering up the chess board and pieces.)* Birds don't get ruptured.
RAVEN. Hell of an ornithologist you'd make.
REBECK. *(Sitting down to eat.)* Hungry?
RAVEN. I don't eat with an audience. Makes me feel like I'm in one of those goddamn Disney nature flicks.
REBECK. Since when am I an audience?
RAVEN. Not you. That group at the gate.

(REBECK stands up suddenly to look and spills the chess pieces and board again. HE sounds excitedly pleased.)

REBECK. Is it a funeral?
RAVEN. No, it's the Macy's Parade. Of course it's a funeral.

REBECK. Thank God. This is just what we needed. It's been too long since we had company. *(HE gathers up the baloney and chess paraphernalia and exits into the mausoleum.)*

RAVEN. You wanted company, you should've joined the "Y."

REBECK. *(Offstage)* Is it a man or a woman?

RAVEN. It's a box.

REBECK. *(Re-entering with his "funeral clothes.")* I'd better hurry. Sometimes they show up before the service is even over. Which way are they headed?

RAVEN. To the Catholic section.

REBECK. A Catholic? Oh, God, they're the worst. They expect so much.

[Music Cue #2: PROLOGUE]

RAVEN. So learn Latin.

REBECK.

I HOPE THAT THIS ONE IS FRIENDLY.
AND NOT AFRAID TO TAKE ADVICE.

RAVEN. Which won't stop you from giving it.

REBECK.

I HOPE THAT THIS ONE HAS EDUCATION,
WIT, AND IMAGINATION.
AND UNDER FORTY WOULD BE NICE.

RAVEN. "Old man seeks young ghost…"

REBECK.

I HOPE THAT THIS ONE
IS FULL OF MYST'RIES
AND SECRETS TO CONFESS.
AND, OF COURSE, HE *MUST* PLAY CHESS.
OH, YES!

(REBECK exits, dressed for work, literally running off with all the enthusiasm and excitement of a child.)

RAVEN. *(Calling after him.)* Be careful now. Keep to the back. And don't speak to anyone you can't see through. *(Sighs to himself.)* Here we go again.

(The stage goes suddenly to BLACK.)

ACT I

Scene 1

(The stage is in DARKNESS. A shaft of LIGHT appears on MICHAEL, propped up as if in a coffin, center stage. It hits his face. [Music Cue #3: I'M NOT GOING GENTLY] There is a "stinger" in the orchestra as his eyes fly open. Wide.)

MICHAEL. Sandra? God, I just had the worst dream. (*HE stops as, reaching for her, his hand hits the unseen coffin lid. HE tests the lid.*) Sandra? Why is there a lid on the bed?
MICHAEL MORGAN, YOU'RE A FOOL.
THIS IS NOTHING,
JUST A NIGHTMARE. DAMMIT, SANDRA, WAKE
  ME UP!
ANYONE CAN WAKE UP FROM A NIGHTMARE;
YOU'VE ONLY GOTTA GIVE YOURSELF A PINCH.

(And HE does. But nothing changes.)

JUST PINCH AN INCH AND IT'S A CINCH.

(We hear the murmuring voice of a PRIEST.)

VOICE OF PRIEST. Ashes to ashes. Dust to dust.
MICHAEL. I really don't like this dream.
VOICE OF PRIEST. Into Thy hands, oh Lord, we commend the spirit of Thy servant, Michael Morgan.

(A WOMAN sobs theatrically.)

MICHAEL. My analyst would love it.

VOICE OF PRIEST. (*With soft female sobbing under.*) In the name of the Father, the Son, and the Holy Ghost.
MICHAEL. If I had an analyst.
VOICE OF PRIEST. Amen.

(*With a lurch, the COFFIN tilts.*)

MICHAEL. I'll get one.

(*It lurches again. We hear the sound of SQUEAKING PULLEYS as it is lowered into the grave.*)

KEEP YOUR COOL AND
KEEP YOUR WITS,
NOW YOU'RE IN A PICKLE.
IF, GOD FORBID, THE DAMN THING HITS,
YOU'RE NOT WORTH A NICKEL.
PEOPLE NEVER HIT THE GROUND.
NOT IN DREAMS.
WHEN THEY FALL,
THEN THEY WAKE UP SAFE IN BED.
IF YOU DON'T YOU'RE—

(*The COFFIN lands with a thud.*)

DEAD.

(*We hear the sound of DIRT being shoveled onto the coffin lid.*)

MICHAEL. No! Wait! There's been a mistake!! You can't do this to me. I've got a whole life left in front of me!!!

(*Dead silence. Finally.*)

GUESS IT'S TIME TO FACE THE TRUTH.

THIS IS MUCH MORE THAN A NIGHTMARE.
IN THE FLOWER OF MY YOUTH,
I'VE BEEN PLUCKED!
LOOK, I KNOW YOU THINK YOU'RE PERFECT.
AND WHO AM I TO SAY IT ISN'T SO?
BUT IF I REALLY HAVE TO GO,
I'M NOT GOING GENTLY.
THERE'S TOO MUCH I DIDN'T DO.
FINISH TOLSTOI.
VISIT CLEVELAND.
WIN A PULITZER OR TWO.
I'VE NO DOUBT THERE'S LESSONS TO BE
   LEARNED HERE,
BUT, FRANKLY, SO FAR ALL I'VE COME TO
   KNOW
IS WHY I'VE ALWAYS HATED POE!
SO I'M NOT GOING GENTLY.
34—YOU SIMPLY CAN'T!
34 IS JOKING.
FOR THIS I HAD A HAIR TRANSPLANT
AND I GAVE UP SMOKING?!
EV'RYBODY MAKES MISTAKES.
BE A SPORT.
TAKE ONE BACK.
WAKE ME UP IN BED ALIVE.

(HE closes his eyes and starts to count.)

   ONE, TWO, THREE, FOUR,—

(The EYES open. Nothing is changed.)

   Shit.
LISTEN,
AREN'T YOU DOING SOMETHING WRONG HERE?
OKAY, THE BODY MAY BELONG HERE,
BUT THE SOUL'S ANOTHER THING.
HEY THERE,

WHILE YOU FLOUNDER FOR A PUNCHLINE,
WORMS ARE FORMING IN A LUNCHLINE
PLANNING MORGAN A LA KING.
LET ME OUT.
FIND A HOUSE I CAN HAUNT AND
GET ME OUT!
I AM NOT
GONNA SQUAT
IN THIS PLOT
'TIL I ROT! NO, I'M NOT!!

(Still no response.)

AREN'T YOU GLAD WE CLEARED THE AIR?
ARE YOU READY?
'CAUSE I'M WAITING.
ISN'T ANYBODY THERE?
ISN'T ANYONE THERE?!

Saaaandraaaaa!!!!

*(And with incredible abruptness, HE is out.
REBECK steps forward out of the background .)*

REBECK. She's gone, I'm afraid. You were rather late in showing up.

(MICHAEL stares at him.)

REBECK. Most people just sort of sprout. Like a geranium.
MICHAEL. Are you talking to me?
REBECK. The name is Rebeck. Jonathan Rebeck.
MICHAEL. *(With relief.)* Michael Morgan—*(HE stops short in horror as his hand goes right through REBECK's. HE snatches the hand away as if burned.)* I'm really dead, aren't I?

REBECK. It's all right. It happens to everyone. This way.

(HE starts to walk through the cemetery. MICHAEL scrambles to follow.)

MICHAEL. Hey!
REBECK. It was a fine funeral. Your wife never once stopped crying.
MICHAEL. So I heard.
REBECK. A bit sparsely attended. Was it a sudden death?
MICHAEL. Where are we going?
REBECK. Not far.
MICHAEL. For that matter, where are we? This can't be heaven.
REBECK. No.
MICHAEL. What's the verdict then? Hell or purgatory?
REBECK. Actually, it's the Bronx.
MICHAEL. That bad.
REBECK. You're in Yorkchester Cemetery. Heaven or hell is up to you.

(THEY arrive at the mausoleum. The RAVEN is perched on top.)

MICHAEL. You mean this is it?
REBECK. Yes. Do you play chess?
MICHAEL. Chess?
REBECK. *(With a sigh.)* No one does anymore. I don't know what the world is coming to. Oh well, I can teach you.
MICHAEL. Chess.
REBECK. I'll get the board. Now you stay right there.

(And HE goes into the mausoleum. MICHAEL stares after. Then, nearly into the ear of the RAVEN:)

MICHAEL. HEEEELLLLLPPPPP!
RAVEN. You'll need it.

(MICHAEL leaps back in surprise.)

RAVEN. He cheats.
MICHAEL. You can speak!
RAVEN. I used to be able to hear, too.
MICHAEL. Let me outta here.

(HE heads off as REBECK emerges with the board.)

REBECK. Where do you think you're going?
MICHAEL. To get some answers.
REBECK. I'm the only one who can give you answers.
RAVEN. He's not gonna like 'em. He's trouble.
MICHAEL. Who *are* you? Or is *were* you more socially correct?
REBECK. Oh, I'm not a ghost. I'm just a man. I'm alive.
MICHAEL. *(Pointing to the mausoleum.)* But you went in there.
REBECK. I live in there.
MICHAEL. What kind of a man lives in a mausoleum?
RAVEN. A cheap one.
REBECK. I have a gift. For communicating with the dead. Where else would I live?
MICHAEL. How long have you been here?
REBECK. About twenty years, I guess. One loses track. Now, this is a pawn.
MICHAEL. I know how to play chess.
REBECK. Well why didn't you say so?

MICHAEL. What I *want* to know is what's going to happen to me!

REBECK. You're not ready—

MICHAEL. No answers, no chess.

RAVEN. *(With a squawk.)* No class.

REBECK *(After a moment.)* Nothing happens. At first. You see, only the body dies quickly. The soul hangs on.

RAVEN. Like an amputation. You itch like hell, but there's nothing left to scratch.

MICHAEL. Can we lose the crow?

RAVEN. Raven, you asshole, raven.

MICHAEL. What about later?

REBECK. You begin to forget things. Little things at first. The smell of coffee. What it felt like to clip your toenails. All the things you can no longer have. Or do.

MICHAEL. How long before it all goes?

REBECK. That depends—

MICHAEL. On what?

RAVEN. On how much of a shit you've been.

REBECK. It depends on what you still have to work through.

MICHAEL. What do you mean?

REBECK. You have to come to terms, Michael. With your life, yourself. A month is about average.

MICHAEL. And then?

REBECK. You disappear. I don't know any more. I wish I did.

MICHAEL. Self-annihilation. How appropriate.

REBECK. Oh, no. You have it all wrong. [Music Cue #4: MUCH MORE ALIVE] Think of it as a resolution. A culmination.

EV'RYONE WHO ARRIVES HERE
HAS A JOB THEY HAVE TO DO.
FREE, AT LAST, OF THEIR EARTHLY DRIVES HERE,
THEY RE-APPRAISE THEIR LIVES HERE,
AND I MAKE SURE THEY SEE IT THROUGH.

HELP THEM SORT
THROUGH THE LONG AND SHORT
OF A LIFETIME SEEN ANEW.
GRANTED GREATER PERSPECTIVE,
HERE THEY FIND THEY CAN EXPLORE
FAR BEYOND WHAT THE HUMAN EYE SEES,
'TIL THEY CAN FACE THE CRISES
THEY COULD NEVER FACE BEFORE.
TO HELP A SOUL
TO BE HEALED AND WHOLE
IS A JOURNEY RICH AND RARE.
NOTHING ELSE CAN COMPARE.
IT'S MUCH MORE ALIVE.
SO MUCH MORE ALIVE.
THAN THE PETTY WORLD OF THE FLESH,
WHERE CONFUSIONS ESPECIALLY THRIVE.
YES, MUCH MORE ALIVE.
HERE YOU'LL FIND INESSENTIALS
EFFORTLESSLY FALL AWAY.
UNENCUMBERED WITH BLAME OR PITY,
WE REACH THE NITTY GRITTY.
(AS THE YOUNG ONES LIKE TO SAY.)
MAKING SENSE
OF A LIFE'S EVENTS
IS WHAT ALL OF THIS IS FOR.
YOU'LL DISCOVER THAT YOU'RE
MUCH MORE ALIVE.
SO MUCH MORE ALIVE.
NOW THAT FINALLY YOU ARE FREED
OF THE TERRIBLE NEED TO SURVIVE.
YES, MUCH MORE ALIVE.

    MICHAEL. *My* life is *my* business, old man. Keep out of it.

    REBECK. *(With firm, but fatherly remonstrance.)* Michael.

WE ALL HARBOR SECRETS
WE FIERCELY PROTECT.
EMOTIONS WE'D RATHER DENY

THAN DISSECT.
AND THEY STAY LOCKED AWAY.
NOW IS THE HOUR
AND HERE IS THE PLACE
TO GATHER YOUR NERVE
AND FACE UP TO THE FACE
THAT YOU KNEW WASN'T YOU.
SEEING IT CLEARLY IS THE KEY.
IF YOU NEED A MIRROR,
USE ME.
    MICHAEL. All I need is a cab.
    REBECK. How did you die, Michael?
    MICHAEL. I'm going home.
    REBECK. You can't. You have to stay where you're buried. At least until you …
    MICHAEL. Forget things. I remember. But what if you refuse to forget?
    RAVEN. This could take years.
    MICHAEL. What if you just hold on?!
    REBECK. The harder you resist, the longer you stay.
    MICHAEL. Bingo!
    REBECK. I knew you weren't ready.
EV'RYONE WHO ARRIVES HERE,
TRAVELS ON INTO THE NIGHT.
THERE IS LITTLE THAT YOU CAN LEARN, E-
LECTING TO MAKE THE JOURNEY
WHILE PUTTING UP A HOPELESS FIGHT.
TAKING STOCK CAN BE QUITE A SHOCK,
AH, BUT ONCE YOU KNOW THE SCORE,
YOU CAN'T BE HURT ANYMORE!
AND YOU'LL BE ALIVE.
MORE TRULY ALIVE.
HAVING DONE AWAY WITH THE LIES
WE ALL USE AS A RUSE TO SURVIVE.
OH, SO MUCH MORE ALIVE!

(Suddenly, the RAVEN squawks loudly.)

REBECK. What is it? What's wrong?
RAVEN. Shh!! There's a woman over there.
MICHAEL. What?
REBECK. Has she seen me?
RAVEN. Not yet.

(REBECK begins to gather things up.)

MICHAEL. What are you doing?
REBECK. I resign.
MICHAEL. Don't you want to talk to her?
REBECK. No.
MICHAEL. Well I do.
RAVEN. Well *you* can't.
MICHAEL. *(To REBECK.)* Is that true?
REBECK. Yes.
MICHAEL. But I can talk to you.
REBECK. I told you, Michael. I'm different. I have a gift.
RAVEN. She's closing in, Rebeck.
MICHAEL. You do it for me then. Be my medium.
REBECK. Don't be foolish.
MICHAEL. I want to talk with somebody alive!
RAVEN. Jewish widow, twelve o'clock high!
REBECK. No, Michael. If I'm caught they'll throw me out of here. And I can't go outside. I never go outside.

(REBECK moves to the mausoleum door. MICHAEL speaks sharply.)

MICHAEL. Rebeck, don't.

(REBECK stiffens with his hand on the door.)

MICHAEL. She's looking this way. She'll see you go in.

RAVEN. Go in!
MICHAEL. A strange looking man with a chessboard breaking into a mausoleum? She'll report it, Rebeck. She looks very respectable.

(Slowly, REBECK turns around. HE comes back to the board and sets up the pieces.)

RAVEN. Ah, Rebeck, you're such a schmuck.

(KLAPPER enters. SHE has already spotted REBECK and is advancing toward him.)

MICHAEL. Better call her over. Who knows what she saw? Or what she's thinking? *(Calling to KLAPPER.)* Good afternoon! *(Back to REBECK.)* Come on, Rebeck. Live a little.
RAVEN. You're gonna have to get yourself out of this one.

Scene 2

(And HE hops behind the mausoleum. REBECK remains fixed on the chessboard, hoping against hope that SHE won't disturb him.)

KLAPPER. Hello.
MICHAEL. Whaddaya say to that?
KLAPPER. So who's winning?
MICHAEL. You are, lady.
KLAPPER. Lovely day.
MICHAEL. The woman's a tiger. *(Pause.)* Speak up, Rebeck. Be forgettable or she'll report you.
KLAPPER. Perfect for chess.

(REBECK grunts.)

KLAPPER. It should stay like this, is all I ask.

(REBECK grunts.)

KLAPPER. You do this a lot?

(REBECK grunts.)

MICHAEL. Keep this up and she'll have you committed.
REBECK. It was such a lovely day, I couldn't stay indoors.
KLAPPER. I know. I was up in my apartment this morning and I said to myself, Gertrude, such a day you should share with Morris. Morris shouldn't think nobody remembered him on such a day. Morris is my husband. Morris Klapper. You know, Morris in the big house. *(SHE points in the direction SHE came.)*
MICHAEL. House?
KLAPPER. All marble. Even inside. Morris likes marble.
MICHAEL. Lucky stiff.
KLAPPER. I don't care what the rabbi says. Why should the goyim get all the glory?
MICHAEL. Why, indeed?
KLAPPER. He deserves a house. My Morris was a good man.
MICHAEL. Say something, Rebeck.
REBECK. Yes. *(He looks up at KLAPPER for the first time.)* He was. A good man.
MICHAEL. He means ghost.
KLAPPER. *(Thrilled.)* You knew him?!
REBECK. No!
KLAPPER. But you just said—
REBECK. I mean yes. Sort of. Hardly.
KLAPPER. How did you know him?
MICHAEL. In passing.

REBECK. We played chess. In a tournament. Once.
KLAPPER. So what's your name?
MICHAEL. *(Whispering into Rebeck's ear.)* Rebeck.
REBECK. Rebeck. Jonathan Rebeck.
KLAPPER. It's Jewish?
REBECK. Yes.
KLAPPER. *(Pleased.)* I thought so.
MICHAEL. Stop flirting and ask her how the Yankees are doing.
KLAPPER. This isn't the Jewish section.
REBECK. This plot belongs to a friend of mine. His family died out.
MICHAEL. Better yet, get her recipe for ruggelah.
REBECK. I'm the last who remembers.
KLAPPER. I'm sorry. I know what that's like. A year and two months now Morris is dead, and I still keep leaning over to wake him up in the morning. *(Pause.)* For a moment, I even thought you were him.
MICHAEL. Whoa!
KLAPPER. I came over the hill and saw you there and my first thought was, "Klapper, my God, there's Morris."
MICHAEL. This record is broken.
REBECK. I'm sorry.
KLAPPER. For what? It was a nice moment.
REBECK. I was only working on a chess problem.
KLAPPER. You and Morris.
MICHAEL. To hell with Morris.

[Music Cue #5: YOU AND MORRIS]

REBECK. I love the quiet here.
KLAPPER.
YOU AND MORRIS.
MICHAEL. Morris is dead.
REBECK. I can concentrate.

KLAPPER.
YOU AND MORRIS.

MICHAEL. I want to hear about life!

KLAPPER.	**MICHAEL.**
MORRIS USED TO DO THIS ALL THE TIME. PLAYING CHESS IN A CORNER BY HIMSELF. AND I'D SAY— MORRIS!!	Please! Rebeck! Do something. This is not what I had in mind. Stop her! You've got to stop her!! REBECK!!!!

REBECK. *(In spite of himself.)* MICHAEL!!!

KLAPPER. *(After a beat, a little anxiously.)* You feel all right?

REBECK. I … I thought I heard someone.

(A silence. Then it dawns on KLAPPER.)

KLAPPER. Your friend, huh?

REBECK. *(Terrified. Does she see MICHAEL?)* My friend?

(MICHAEL steps forward eagerly.)

KLAPPER. Your friend. *(SHE points past MICHAEL.)* The one in there.

(MICHAEL sags visibly.)

REBECK. Oh. Yes. Michael. Michael …

MICHAEL. Morgan.

REBECK. *(Sneaking a look at the mausoleum name.)* Wilder. Very old friend. Ev'ry now and then I'm sure I hear him calling me.

MICHAEL. Judas.

KLAPPER. You were close with this friend?

REBECK. Like brothers.

MICHAEL. This is useless.

KLAPPER. You want to know something?

MICHAEL. I'm outta here.

(MICHAEL starts off. REBECK speaks to him.)

REBECK. No!
KLAPPER. *(Shaken.)* Okay!

(MICHAEL is gone.)

REBECK. I mean yes. Yes, I'd like to know.
KLAPPER. Sometimes I hear Morris, too. *(Confidentially, with some embarrassment.)* Do they talk about you?
REBECK. What?
KLAPPER. They talk about me. All I gotta do is walk in a room and it starts to sound like laying time at the hen house. [Music Cue #6: YOU KNOW WHAT I MEAN] You shouldn't let it bother you. They don't know.
"CRAZY KLAPPER,"
THAT'S WHAT THEY CALL ME.
AT THE GRAVEYARD DAY AFTER DAY.
LOST A HUSBAND
AND ALL HER MARBLES.
WELL, WHO CARES WHAT THEY SAY?
MORRIS KLAPPER.
GAVE ME A LIFETIME.
THIRTY YEARS TOGETHER WE HAD.
HOW COULD I ABANDON MY MORRIS?
IF I EVER HAD TO,
THEN I *WOULD* GO MAD.
HOW COULD I LEAVE HIM?
HE'S ALL ALONE HERE,
WITH NO ONE TO KEEP
ALL THE SILENCE AT BAY.
I WON'T FORGET HIM
AND HE SHOULD KNOW IT.
THE MEM'RIES REMAIN EVERGREEN.

BUT YOU KNOW WHAT I MEAN.
OTHER WIDOWS
BRUSH UP THEIR TYPING.
TAKE A JOB AND TRY NOT TO GRIEVE.
OTHER WIDOWS
LEARN HOW TO TANGO
EV'RY THURSDAY EV'NING.
I DON'T HAVE TO
BRUSH UP MY TYPING.
MORRIS LEFT ENOUGH TO GET THROUGH.
I DON'T NEED TO
LEARN HOW TO TANGO.
THAT REQUIRES TWO
AND TWO WOULD NEVER DO.
HOW COULD I LEAVE HIM?
IF I COULD LEAVE HIM,
I'D NO LONGER BE
WHO HE LOVED ALL HIS LIFE.
I'M MAKING CERTAIN
THAT WHEN I JOIN HIM
NO CHANGES WILL COME IN BETWEEN.
BUT YOU KNOW WHAT I MEAN.
MORRIS WASN'T HANDSOME
OR FORCEFUL OR BRILLIANT.
HE WAS NEVER WHAT WE THOUGHT OF AS A
   "CATCH."
I WAS NEVER PRETTY
OR GRACEFUL OR CHARMING,
BUT I TELL YOU, THERE WAS NEVER SUCH A
   MATCH!
ALWAYS "MORRIS AND HIS GERTRUDE,"
ALWAYS "GERTRUDE AND HER MORRIS."
NO DIVISIONS.
NO RESENTMENTS.
NO CHILDREN,
BUT NO ONE HAS EV'RYTHING.
NEVER SORRY
EVEN ONCE!

WHEN YOU'RE ONLY TWO,
IT'S LOVE THAT MAKES THE GLUE.
You must think I'm crazy too, running on and on like this.
REBECK. Oh no. Not at all. Not at all.
KLAPPER. *(With a smile of relief.)*
SUCH A PLEASURE
SITTING AND TALKING
WITH A KINDRED SPIRIT LIKE YOU.
IT'S A GIFT TO KNOW HOW TO LISTEN,
FOUND IN VERY FEW.
MY MORRIS HAD IT, TOO.
HOW COULD I LEAVE HIM?
I WOULDN'T KNOW
WHAT TO DO,
WHERE TO GO,
HOW TO LIVE,
HOW TO BE.
I'LL NEVER LEAVE HIM,
AND IF THAT'S CRAZY,
THEN CRAZY IS ALL RIGHT WITH ME.
I DON'T CARE HOW I'M SEEN.
BUT YOU KNOW WHAT I MEAN.
My sister Ida, she lives underneath me, she's always after me to move to Miami with her. I told her, "Ida, I lived thirty year's in our father's house and thirty years in my husband's house. You'd never get rid of me."

(The roar of an approaching TRUCK interrupts Klapper's story. REBECK looks up in a panic.)

REBECK. Oh, my God, it's Campos! *(HE scrambles up. KLAPPER looks puzzled.)* The gatekeeper!

(And HE dashes behind the mausoleum. KLAPPER stares in amazement. We hear the voice of CAMPOS from off-stage.)

CAMPOS. Hey! Lady! It's closing time. Move it. You want to spend a night with the spooks?
KLAPPER. *(Still riveted on the hidden REBECK.)* Keep your shirt on.
CAMPOS. You got fifteen minutes. Then I lock the gate.

(And the TRUCK roars off. REBECK re-emerges. KLAPPER waits for the explanation.)

REBECK. He makes me nervous.
KLAPPER. You must have one heck of a time on the subway. Well, come on. "You want to spend a night with the spooks?"
REBECK. I'm not going. Yet.
KLAPPER. Oh? You planning a nice climb over the fence, maybe?
REBECK. *(Madly inventing.)* I have to get my watch.
KLAPPER. Your watch?
REBECK. My watch. I left it in the men's room. At the other end of the cemetery.
KLAPPER. Again like Morris. Absent minded. So let's go.
REBECK. There isn't time. You'll get locked in. *(HE starts to dash off. Stops and turns.)* I enjoyed talking with you. Very much. Goodbye.

(And HE is gone. KLAPPER stares in bewilderment. Then SHE notices the chessboard.)

KLAPPER. Hey Rebeck! Don't forget your chessboard! Rebeck!! *(But HE doesn't respond. To herself.)* You and Morris. *(SHE starts off, then stops. Impulsively, SHE rummages through her purse, pulls out pen and paper, and scribbles something down. SHE leaves it under a chess piece.)* You know what I mean.

[Music Cue #6a: KLAPPER'S EXIT]

(And SHE exits. The RAVEN emerges from behind the mausoleum. HE looks at the note, then after REBECK.)

RAVEN. Schmuck.

(HE flies off cawing as we move to:)

[Music Cue #6b: LAURA AT THE GATE]

Scene 3

(The cemetery gate. LAURA enters. SHE looks around in detached curiosity. SHE goes over to the gate. SHE cannot pass. Undisturbed, SHE moves away. MICHAEL strides on. HE heads directly for the gate. Unable to pass, HE continues to try. LAURA stops him.)

LAURA. It's no use. You can't go through. They've locked us in.

(MICHAEL turns. HE stares at her in amazement.)

LAURA. Hello. I'm Laura. Laura Durand.
MICHAEL. There is a God.
LAURA. There is? Where? *(SHE looks behind her. Then SHE laughs.)* Oh. You're just glad to see me.
MICHAEL. How long have you been here? What do you know about this place?
LAURA. I'm afraid I've only just arrived. I probably know less than you do.
MICHAEL. Who cares? You're the only one I've met so far in this madhouse who's … like me.

[Music Cue #6c: DISAPPEARANCE CUES]

(LAURA's SPOTLIGHT goes out.)

MICHAEL. Hey! Where'd you go?
LAURA. What?
MICHAEL. Come back!
LAURA. I haven't gone anywhere.
MICHAEL. I can't see you.
LAURA. But I'm right here.
MICHAEL. You're just a blob. A feminine blob. But a blob. Try to focus on something. Think about your sexiest dress. Your sheerest pantyhose.
LAURA. I don't wear pantyhose.
MICHAEL. Your rattiest jeans. Whatever. Just concentrate.
LAURA. (*SHE does. Finally.*) Well?
MICHAEL. You're still a bit fuzzy.
LAURA. Well so are you.
MICHAEL. I am not! (*HE concentrates for a moment.*) How's that?
LAURA. I'd say somewhere in between a Monet and a Picasso. I like it. It's different.
MICHAEL. It's terrible! Quick, talk to me. Tell me about your life.
LAURA. Why?
MICHAEL. So I can remember about living.
LAURA. Are you sure you want to?
MICHAEL. It's the only way to hold on. You have to remember. Otherwise you disappear. Like all of them. Maybe you go to sleep. Maybe you just cease to exist. I don't know and I don't want to find out.
LAURA. There's really nothing to tell.
MICHAEL. Oh, that's terrific. That's helpful.
LAURA. I'm sorry, but it's true. I was born, grew up, got sick, and promptly died. All in proper sequence. I never saw Europe, read *Ulysses,* kept a lover ... I never got around to it.

MICHAEL. I must have faded a good fifty watts just listening to that.

LAURA. Look, if it's that important, why don't you tell me about you? What's worth remembering about your life?

MICHAEL. My writing career, for one. Sweating blood over a turn of phrase. Getting a rave in the Sunday Times. Posing for the dust jacket. Dinner at Mailer's. Not to mention sex, drugs, and rock and roll.

LAURA. It's working. You're practically an Andy Warhol now. Keep going.

MICHAEL. What else? Well, I taught a little. And then there was Sandra. I could hardly forget Sandra.

LAURA. Sandra?

MICHAEL. My wife.

LAURA. Oh. *(SHE peers at him closely.)* I think you're about as solid as you're going to get.

MICHAEL. You're looking better yourself.

LAURA. So you were a writer? I always wanted to write. All I could ever manage was some bad poetry. And a job in a bookstore. Phoenix Books. Used, of course. What did you write?

MICHAEL. Difficult novels. Except for one. *The Velvet Abyss*. It was almost a best seller. Maybe you read it?

LAURA. *The Velvet Abyss*? I don't think so.

MICHAEL. By Michael Morgan.

LAURA. Michael Morgan?

MICHAEL. You have read it.

LAURA. No. But I've heard the name.

MICHAEL. The name is common. If you don't know the book …

LAURA. Ah well, it doesn't matter.

MICHAEL. Yes it does.

LAURA. Well, I can't remember.

MICHAEL. You aren't even trying.

LAURA. How do you know?

MICHAEL. All I have to do is look.

LAURA. Well maybe I don't want to.
MICHAEL. You have to! Giving up the fight is death.
LAURA. I know that. *(Pause.)* I know all about that.
MICHAEL. Then, for God's sake Laura, help me.
LAURA. Why?
MICHAEL. I can't do it alone. I need help. I need you.

[Music Cue #7: A FINE AND PRIVATE PLACE]

LAURA. No you don't.
YOUR LIFE MAY WELL BE A LIFE TO REMEMBER.
YOUR LIFE MAY WELL BE THE ENVY OF
  EV'RYONE.
MAYBE YOU'VE GOT TO HOLD ON TO IT.
WELL, YOU CAN GO RIGHT AHEAD.
I'M OFF TO BED.
MINE WAS A LIFE I'VE NO WISH TO REMEMBER.
MY LIFE WAS NEVER THE ENVY OF ANYONE.
WHY SHOULD I TRY TO HOLD ON TO IT?
GO ON AND PUT UP YOUR FIGHT.
I'D RATHER PUT OUT THE LIGHT.
A FINE AND PRIVATE PLACE,
THAT'S WHAT THE GRAVE SHOULD BE.
A FINAL, WARM EMBRACE
TO SET ME FREE.
FREE.
FREE OF MY LONGINGS AND
FREE OF MY FAILINGS.
FREE OF DESIRE.
FREE OF HOPING
THAT SOMEDAY IT ALL WOULD SEEM POSSIBLE.
LIFE WAS EXHAUSTING AT BEST.
I NEED A PLACE I CAN REST.
A FINE AND PRIVATE PLACE
WHERE ALL DESIRE DIES.
A DARK AND QUIET PLACE

TO CLOSE MY EYES.
   MICHAEL. Wise. Very wise.
I JUST DON'T BELIEVE YOU.
   LAURA. You don't.
   MICHAEL. No, I don't.
LAURA, WE'RE YOUNG.
WE'RE BOTH OF US YOUNG.
THERE'S SO MUCH WE'LL NEVER KNOW.
   LAURA. I'm content.
   MICHAEL.
HOW CAN YOU SIT THERE
AND SAY THAT YOU'RE WILLING
TO LET IT ALL GO?
   LAURA. It already went.
   MICHAEL.
WE STILL HAVE A CHANCE,
ONE FINAL CHANCE
FOR A LITTLE MORE TIME.
   LAURA. Not me.
   MICHAEL.
HELP ME REMEMBER
AND LET ME HELP YOU.
   LAURA. No.
   MICHAEL.
IT'S THE LEAST YOU CAN DO.
   LAURA. No!
   MICHAEL.
THE LEAST YOU CAN DO.
   LAURA.
WHY SHOULD I LISTEN TO YOU?
MY LIFE IS THROUGH.
KEEP TO YOURSELF
WITH YOUR HUNGER FOR LIVING.
KEEP TO YOURSELF
WITH YOUR LONGING FOR MEMORY.
I CAN'T SUPPLY YOU WITH MEMORIES.
I NEVER LEARNED HOW TO LIVE,
SO I HAVE NOTHING TO GIVE.

LAURA.	**MICHAEL.**
A FINE AND PRIVATE PLACE	LAURA, WE'RE YOUNG,
THAT'S WHAT MY GRAVE WILL BE.	WE'RE BOTH OF US YOUNG.
A FINAL, WARM EMBRACE	WE STILL HAVE A CHANCE.
WILL SET ME FREE.	ONE FINAL CHANCE.

MICHAEL. Laura—

LAURA.
I WILL BE FREE.

MICHAEL.
LAURA, HOW SAD, HOW HONESTLY SAD.
YOU CAN'T MISS WHAT YOU'VE NEVER HAD.
YOU HAVE EV'RY RIGHT TO BE ROYALLY PISSED,
BUT DON'T CEASE TO EXIST
'TIL YOU KNOW WHAT YOU'VE MISSED!

LAURA. I didn't think you would understand.

MICHAEL. How old *were* you? 42? 96?

LAURA. *Thirty*-two.

MICHAEL. And you have no regrets. You aren't hungry for all the things you wanted? What were they? *Ulysses*, Europe … love?

LAURA. No.

MICHAEL. You're not through with life, you're afraid of it.

[Music Cue #8: AS LONG AS I CAN]

LAURA. We're *not* alive!

MICHAEL. Nonsense.
AS LONG AS I CAN BRISTLE
AT BEING TOLD I'M THROUGH,
AS LONG AS I CAN WHISTLE
THE *RHAPSODY IN BLUE*.
AS LONG AS I CAN WONDER

HOW ANYONE COULD WELCOME THIS BLUN-
  DER,
I'LL NEVER FADE POLITELY FROM VIEW.
AS LONG AS I HAVE QUESTIONS
I HAVEN'T ANSWERED YET,
AS LONG AS I STILL WORRY
ABOUT THE OZONE THREAT,
AS LONG AS I'M UNCERTAIN
WHAT'S ON THE OTHER SIDE OF THE CURTAIN,
I'M GRABBING ALL THE ROPE I CAN GET.
SCRAPS OF LIVING
CROWD MY SENSES:
JOURNEYING TO OZ,
VANILLA HAAGEN-DAZS,
THE SUDDEN CHILL OF AN AUTUMN EV'NING,
THE FLOODING WARMTH OF A LOVERS' KISS,
I REFUSE
TO EXCHANGE THEM FOR THIS.
I MAY BE JUST AN EMBER
AND NEVERMORE A FLAME,
BUT WHILE I STILL REMEMBER
THE RHYTHMS OF MY NAME,
WHILE I AM STILL COHERENT,
ALTHOUGH I MAY BE SLIGHTLY TRANSPARENT,
AS FAR AS I'M CONCERNED,
I'M STAYING A MAN
JUST AS LONG AS I CAN.

LAURA. How did you die?

MICHAEL. Why does everyone keep asking me that?!

LAURA. You're so unprepared for this. It's sad, in a way.

MICHAEL. You bet I'm unprepared. *(HE takes a dramatic pause.)* I was murdered.

LAURA. What?

MICHAEL. Poisoned. By my wife.

LAURA. Oh my God.

MICHAEL. You could put it that way.

LAURA. Of course. Michael Morgan. It was in all the papers.

MICHAEL. What was?

LAURA. They arrested your wife. First degree murder.

MICHAEL. How about that?

LAURA. You poor man. You must feel terrible.

MICHAEL. I'm feeling better already.

LET ME HELP YOU.

LET ME SHOW YOU.

LAURA, IT'S SO CLEAR

WHY BOTH OF US ARE HERE.

I NEEDED SOMEONE TO EASE MY HUNGER.

YOU NEEDED SOMEONE TO END YOUR FAST.

IT'S A MATCH.

IT'S A MARRIAGE TO LAST.

AS LONG AS YOU HAVE FEELINGS

THAT YOU COULD NEVER SHOW,

AS LONG AS I HAVE SECRETS

THAT EVEN I DON'T KNOW,

AS LONG AS WE'RE UNITED,

ALTHOUGH THE WRONG CAN NEVER BE
  RIGHTED,

IN SOME WAYS YOU COULD SAY

LIFE JUST BEGAN.

LET'S KEEP IT STRONG

JUST AS LONG AS WE CAN!

AS LONG AS WE CAN.

LAURA. I'm sorry, Michael. Really, I am. But I can't help you. I wouldn't know how. Goodnight.

[Music Cue #8a: LAURA DISAPPEARS]

MICHAEL. Wait. Laura! Don't go. You're wrong, Laura! I need you. Laura!!

(But SHE has disappeared. SHE stands watching him with longing as HE calls to her. Thinking HE sees her

in the distance, HE runs off in pursuit. Sadly, SHE exits in the opposite direction. A SHADOW flies across the sky. We hear the RAVEN caw.)

Scene 4

(The RAVEN lands on the mausoleum. HE drops a McDonalds bag on the steps.)

RAVEN. Damn place oughta have a runway.
MICHAEL. (*Enters.*) Jonathan! Jonathan!!
RAVEN. (*With mocking mimicry.*) He's not here! He's not here!! The one night I bring him a hot meal, too.
MICHAEL. (*Notices the bag.*) You brought that?
RAVEN. I got lucky. Some overworked housewife sent her kid out for the family dinner. (*Chuckles.*) She's never gonna believe him. (*Pause.*) Don't worry, she'll be back.
MICHAEL. What?
RAVEN. She swallowed it all. Hook, line and murder.
MICHAEL. You don't miss a trick.
RAVEN. Wait 'til she finds out the truth.
MICHAEL. And just what is that supposed to mean?
RAVEN. She's gonna be one spitting spectre.
MICHAEL. You don't know what you're talking about.
RAVEN. Ravens know, Morgan. Didn't you ever hear the expression "A little bird told me?"
MICHAEL. There isn't anything I said that wasn't true. I just simplified things a bit.
RAVEN. Tell it to the judge.
LAURA. (*Enters.*) Hello, Michael. (*Pause.*) Fancy meeting you here.
MICHAEL. I thought you were off to bed.
LAURA. I changed my mind.

MICHAEL. Oh?

LAURA. I was wrong. You asked for help and I walked away. You've had a terrible shock. It was selfish of me to abandon you. I'm sure if I was murdered, I'd need help adjusting, too.

MICHAEL. I don't want to adjust. I want to live. Why is that so hard to understand?

LAURA. I understand, Michael. Really, I do. But it's impossible. You have to accept that.

MICHAEL. Will you stay with me until I do?

LAURA. Well —

MICHAEL. No matter how long it takes?

LAURA. I'll stay as long as you need me.

RAVEN. Better think twice about that one.

LAURA. What?

RAVEN. Even Mary Poppins only stays until the wind changes.

LAURA. He speaks?

MICHAEL. Yeah. But he never makes any sense.

LAURA. What next?

(As if in answer to her question, REBECK enters.)

RAVEN. You're late. It's cold.

REBECK. I was held up. *(HE notices MICHAEL and LAURA.)* Good grief.

MICHAEL. Laura Durand. Jonathan Rebeck.

REBECK. *(To the RAVEN.)* Why didn't you tell me there was another one?

RAVEN. You were busy.

REBECK. *(To LAURA.)* You must excuse me. I've never missed a funeral before.

MICHAEL. Jonathan isn't one of us. He just lives here.

LAURA. Where?

MICHAEL. *(Pointing to the mausoleum.)* In there.

LAURA. You mean, he *lives* here?

REBECK. I have a gift—

LAURA. *(Running roughshod over him.)* Oh, you poor man! You don't have to do this. Look, I have this friend. She works for the Coalition for the Homeless. She could have you out of here in no time.
REBECK. You don't understand—
MICHAEL. Maybe he's had a better idea.
REBECK. *(Warningly.)* Michael—
MICHAEL. Was her noodle pudding all Morris said it was?
LAURA. Who's noodle pudding?
MICHAEL. The widow's.
LAURA. What widow?
MICHAEL. I'll bet she cooks better than the bird. In fact, I'll bet she cooks birds. *(To REBECK.)* C'mon, Jonathan, admit it. You liked her.
REBECK. I'll thank you to be more careful in the future, Michael. She very nearly exposed me.
MICHAEL. Sounds steamy.
LAURA. Just who are we talking about?
MICHAEL. A nice Jewish lady who can't let go of her dead husband. You could help *her,* Rebeck. Or do you discriminate against the living?
LAURA. Did you like her?
REBECK. This conversation is over.
MICHAEL. 'Fess up, Rebeck. I'll bet Morris was nuts about her.
REBECK. For your information, Michael, whenever Gertrude visited *him,* Morris came to play chess with *me,* to get away from *her.* "Gertrude never knows when to quit," he used to say. "She'd worry Solomon into an early grave."
LAURA. But did he love her?
REBECK. Well—
MICHAEL. Well, did he?
REBECK. The next time you want a recipe for ruggelah, Michael, call a deli! *(And with that HE stalks into the mausoleum with his McDonalds' bag and slams the door.)*

LAURA. He's lonely.
RAVEN. No he's not.
LAURA. Maybe we should get them together.
RAVEN. Don't.
MICHAEL. We'll do as we like.
RAVEN. You'll be sorry. (*And HE flies off to perch on the cemetery wall.*)
LAURA. (*To MICHAEL.*) So now what?
MICHAEL. How about an ice cream sundae? Haagen-dazs.
LAURA. I'm not here to help you fight, Michael.
MICHAEL. How about a walk, then? Just to talk.
LAURA. All right.

(*THEY start off together.*)

MICHAEL. Your hair. It's chestnut, isn't it?
LAURA. Sorry. It's just brown. Plain brown.

[Music Cue #9: STOP KIDDING YOURSELF]

(*And THEY exit. The RAVEN stirs on his perch. HE spots something on the ground and jumps down. HE wrestles a worm out of the soil and eats it hungrily, ending with a satisfied belch. REBECK comes out on the mausoleum steps in his nightshirt.*)

RAVEN. Close call with the yenta, huh?
REBECK. Too close.
RAVEN. Better lay low for a while.
REBECK. Why?

(*The RAVEN hops over to the chessboard and indicates Klapper's note. *)

RAVEN. She'll be back.
REBECK. (*Reading the note.*) Oh my God. She left her number.

RAVEN. I tell you, things are getting out of hand around here.

REBECK. She must be very lonely.

RAVEN. Go to bed, Rebeck. Have a nightmare. You'll feel better.

(And with that, the RAVEN spreads his wings wide, tucks his head under, and goes to sleep. REBECK sits.)

REBECK.
WELL, THIS WAS QUITE A DAY
AND THAT WAS QUITE A WOMAN.
IMAGINE FACING HER
RIGHT AFTER WORK EV'RY DAY.
IT'S PERFECTLY CLEAR
WHY MORRIS CAME HERE.
HE ALWAYS SAID, "SHE TRIES TOO HARD."
BUT, AT LEAST, SHE KEEPS ON TRYING.
SHE OUGHT TO SAY GOODBYE
AND GO AND TRY SOMETHING NEW.
HOW HARD COULD IT BE
TO GET HER TO SEE?
STOP KIDDING YOURSELF, THERE'S NOT A
  THING YOU CAN DO LIVING HERE.
SHE ISN'T A GHOST
YOU KNOW WILL SOON DISAPPEAR.
IF YOU TOOK A CRACK,
SHE'D KEEP COMING BACK.
STOP KIDDING YOURSELF.

(LIGHTS up on KLAPPER frenetically vacuuming with a very old, very loud upright. The PHONE rings and SHE leaps for it, tripping over the cord in the process.)

KLAPPER. Hello? (*Pause.*) Oh, it's you, Ida. (*Pause.*) No, I wasn't expecting somebody else. (*Pause.*) Well, I'm sorry if the vacuum is loud down there. It's

old. Just like us. Loud and old. (*Pause.*) I know it's
Thursday. So this week I'll go Friday. Big deal. A little
change never hurt anybody. (*Pause.*) What would Morris
care? Look, Ida, where Morris is they only got *one* day.
And it's forever! Goodbye, Ida. (*And SHE hangs up.*
SHE looks viciously at the phone.)
KLAPPER, YOU ARE SUCH A FOOL,
IDA, OY, WOULD SHE BE SHOCKED!
THINKING HE WAS DIFF'RENT
JUST BECAUSE HE DIDN'T HAVE THE NERVE TO
  SAY,
"YOU'RE FACACT."
SO HE PLAYS A LITTLE CHESS.
SO HE MET YOUR MORRIS ONCE.
HOW COULD YOU HAVE LIKED A MAN
WHOSE CONVERSATION'S MOSTLY MADE OF
  GRUNTS?
STOP KIDDING YOURSELF.
HE NEVER KNEW WHAT YOU MEANT,
NOT AT ALL!
IF HE UNDERSTOOD,
YOU CAN BE SURE HE WOULD CALL.
THE MAN'S HAD A WEEK,
TO LEARN HOW TO SPEAK.
STOP KIDDING YOURSELF.

(*LIGHTS back up on REBECK, who is now dressed and
  sitting at his chessboard deep in thought.*)

REBECK.	**KLAPPER.**

GOD KNOWS WHAT
  SHE THOUGHT.
	GOD KNOWS WHAT HE
	  MUST THINK.

I RAN JUST LIKE A
  RABBIT.
	I *KNOW* WHAT HE
	  MUST THINK!

I WONDER IF SHE
  GUESSED?
	HOW COULD HE EVER
	  THINK THAT OF ME?!

IF SHE SHOULD EVER
  GUESS
	I'D BETTER GO SEE
	  MORRIS.

<table>
<tr><td>OH, LORD, WHAT A
   MESS!</td><td>GO APOLOGIZE TO
   MORRIS!</td></tr>
</table>

(KLAPPER starts to gather her things as if to go out.)

   BOTH.
GET HOLD OF YOURSELF.
IT WAS A NARROW ESCAPE AND THAT'S ALL.
NO DAMAGE IS DONE
AS/SO LONG AS SHE/HE DOESN'T CALL.

<table>
<tr><td>   **REBECK.**</td><td>   **KLAPPER.**</td></tr>
<tr><td>BE CAREFUL AND
   STAY
WELL OUT OF HER
   WAY
AND STOP KIDDING
   YOURSELF.</td><td>IF HE SHOULD BE
   THERE,
JUST GIVE HIM THE
   AIR
AND STOP KIDDING
   YOURSELF.</td></tr>
</table>

(The song ends with the slam of Klapper's DOOR as SHE heads back to the cemetery, while REBECK exits as if to hide.)

[Music Cue #9a: AS LONG AS I CAN (REPRISE)]

Scene 5

(The cemetery wall overlooking the city. MICHAEL and LAURA are deep in conversation. Michael's clothes have changed. Gone are the jeans, sneakers etc. In their place are clothes befitting a literary life. Heavy on the tweeds, perhaps. Certainly an expensive cashmere sweater. Chinos, boaters etc. HE is dressing the part. LAURA is still in the same plain, unflattering, inexpensive dress.)

MICHAEL. Well, what do you think? Like it?

LAURA. Very literary.

MICHAEL. And so easy to care for. Just remember and wear. You should try it.

LAURA. I don't need to. I'm happy just the way I am.

MICHAEL. This was my lucky sweater. I won my American Book award in it. And I always wore it first day of classes. Sandra trashed it when the elbows wore through. In revenge for something. I forget what. I was so furious I slept on the couch for a week.

LAURA. An interesting response.

MICHAEL. It heightened the guilt. Sandra was never very good at guilt. You really had to work at it. *(Pause.)* I'll bet she's improved. You don't avoid life imprisonment without a good show of remorse. Too bad we didn't live in Florida. They'd know what to do with her. *(HE mimes electrocution with childish glee.)*

LAURA. You don't really want her dead, do you?

MICHAEL. Nah. She's got the plot next to mine. *(Pause.)* I should've backed out the minute my mother liked her. I was so sure she wouldn't. Mother disapproved of the untalented.

LAURA. Why *did* you marry her? You haven't said one kind word about her all week.

MICHAEL. Given the circumstances, I think that's understandable.

LAURA. And when do we get to the circumstances?

MICHAEL. Laura—

LAURA. Why won't you talk about it?

MICHAEL. I'd rather not.

LAURA. I've told you lots of things I'd rather not.

MICHAEL. I don't want to discuss it.

LAURA. You've got to. I came back to help you, Michael. But I can't help you if you won't let me.

MICHAEL. It's not very interesting. *(HE pauses to think.)*

LAURA. Don't write it, just tell it.

MICHAEL. What's to tell? She wanted revenge.

LAURA. For?
MICHAEL. A million things.
LAURA. Like?
MICHAEL. I was leaving her. And she didn't take to the idea.
LAURA. Go on.
MICHAEL. I had this novel going. Better than anything I'd ever done. A lot better. And she kept getting in the way. Finally, I had to choose.
LAURA. What was she doing?
MICHAEL. She just never understood what it took. She liked the perks all right. The interviews, the parties, the Hollywood nibbles. But she wanted the work to happen on schedule. Like garbage collection.
LAURA. But why murder? Divorce is so much easier.
MICHAEL. But far less final.
LAURA. But she took such a risk. It doesn't make sense.
MICHAEL. I never said that it did! *(Pause.)* Why do you think I didn't want to talk about it? I can't explain it to myself, much less to you.
LAURA. You have to try.

(KLAPPER enters. A newspaper is in her purse.)

MICHAEL. Well, how about that? Deus ex yenta.
LAURA. What?
MICHAEL. It's the widow Klapper. In, you should pardon the expression, the flesh.
LAURA. Well talk about this later. Do you think she's looking for Jonathan?

(KLAPPER heads purposefully off. THEY follow.)

MICHAEL. She ain't heading for Morris. Want to find out?

LAURA. How? I hate to wound your ego, but she doesn't know you exist.

MICHAEL. I think a little telepathy is in order.

LAURA. I suppose you used to do this sort of thing at parties.

MICHAEL. No, really, it's quite simple. You do it already. How do you speak? You have no tongue, no vocal chords. And yet I understand you. Rebeck understands you. You think it. It just feels like speech to you because that's all you've ever known.

LAURA. Yes, but that's just between us. She's alive.

MICHAEL. True, she can't hear us. But that doesn't mean we can't listen in. [Music Cue #10: THE TELEPATHETIQUE] I do it all the time with visitors. You don't know what you're missing.
IT'S EASY AS IT CAN BE.
IT'S ONE OF THE JOYS OF GHOSTHOOD.
THE THINGS YOU CAN FIND
IN THE MAW OF THE MIND
WILL AMAZE.
AND THE DIRT YOU DREDGE UP'LL
KEEP MEMORY SUPPLE
FOR DAYS.
BE RECKLESS AND FOLLOW ME.
(ANY NORMAL GHOST WOULD.)
EV'RY TRACE OF EMOTION YOU GLEAN
CUTS AS SHARP AND AS CLEAN
AS A KNIFE.
EACH FILLIP AND FRISSON
A DIZZYING SEESAW
OF LIFE!
IT'S MORE THAN A GAME.
IT'S MORE THAN A THRILL.
IT'S FOOD FOR THE SOUL.
IT'S FUEL FOR THE WILL.
IT'S BLESSED ESCAPE
IN PASTURES MORE GREEN.

LAURA. It's obscene! Invading someone's most personal, private thoughts so that you can hang on to life. It's disgusting.

MICHAEL. I knew you'd love it.

LAURA. Have you been listening to my thoughts?!

MICHAEL. Of course not. All I ever get out of you is static.
JUST TRY IT AND YOU'LL AGREE.
IT CERTAINLY DOES A GHOST GOOD.
IT MAY BE IMPROPER
TO BE AN EAVESDROPPER,
BUT, HELL,
YOU KNOW WE WON'T GOSSIP.
JUST WHO COULD WE POSSIBLY TELL?

LAURA. Won't you ever stop fighting?

(By now THEY have reached Rebeck's mausoleum. KLAPPER enters and immediately checks the chess board out. MICHAEL starts in on her. Throughout the song, KLAPPER's actions illustrate Michael's comments.)

MICHAEL. Observe.
KLAPPER, YOU'RE A SCHMUCK
GET SMART AND GET AWAY
WHILE YOUR REPUTATION'S
STILL SECURE.

LAURA. I don't believe this.

MICHAEL.
BUT IF HE LEFT THE BOARD,
THE NOTE WOULD STILL BE THERE.
I'LL BET IT BLEW AWAY.

(Both KLAPPER and MICHAEL make a gesture of excitement.)

MICHAEL.
SURE.

LAURA. You're making a fool of yourself.
MICHAEL.
I GUESS IT COULDN'T HURT,
A COUPLE MINUTES REST.
AND, AFTER ALL, MY FEET
ARE NEARLY NUMB.
LAURA. You really enjoy this, don't you?
MICHAEL.
HOW MUCH YOU WANT TO BET
THEY NEVER CLEAN THESE OFF?
AI, WHAT'S THE DIFF'RENCE?
CLEAN, UNCLEAN,
HERE I COME.

(KLAPPER sits on the steps with a thud. SHE adjusts her bra strap as MICHAEL imitates.)

LAURA. You're shameless.

(KLAPPER starts to rummage in her purse. SHE drops the newspaper on the step. LAURA challenges MICHAEL.)

LAURA. Well?
MICHAEL. The general inspects her troops.

(Sure enough, KLAPPER pulls out a small compact mirror and starts checking herself out.)

MICHAEL.
OH, MY GOD, CAN THAT BE REALLY ME?
SO WHO DID YOU EXPECT, JANE FONDA?

(SHE pulls out some lipstick.)

MICHAEL.
MAYBE JUST A TOUCH OF JUNGLE RED.

(With a sudden look of guilt, SHE stops in mid-application.)

MICHAEL.
LIPSTICK IN A CEMETERY?
KLAPPER!
SUCH A SHONDA.

(KLAPPER closes the lipstick, puts it away, and shuts the purse.)

LAURA. A shonda?
MICHAEL. I just call 'em as I hear 'em.
LAURA. We shouldn't be doing this.
MICHAEL. Which makes it twice as much fun.

(KLAPPER makes a move as if to get up.)

LAURA. Now what?
MICHAEL.
SITTING ON THE STEPS
OF A STRANGER'S HOUSE,
PRIMPING LIKE A SCHOOLGIRL IN A SPIN. IT'S
LACKING IN RESPECT,
UNDIGNIFIED AND WORSE.
I REALLY OUGHT TO GO.

(A moment of consideration.)

FIVE MINUTES.

(SHE settles back down, picks up the paper, and starts leafing through it.)

LAURA. We've got to find him before she goes away.
MICHAEL. No way. He's hiding from her.
LAURA. Well, what are we going to do?

MICHAEL. *(Making the gesture of telepathy.)* I can't *think* of a thing.
LAURA. No.
MICHAEL. Just call him. You don't have to listen in.
LAURA. Michael, you know how I feel about this.

(KLAPPER puts the paper down noisily. SHE begins to stir, rubbing her eyes, stretching. In the process, SHE stands up.)

MICHAEL. T minus 4 and counting.
LAURA. *(Giving in.)* What do I do?
MICHAEL.
YOU JUST HAVE TO CONCENTRATE.
DO NOTHING BUT PICTURE REBECK.
AS SOON AS HE'S CLEAR, YOU
CAN THINK AND HE'LL HEAR YOU
JUST FINE.

(LAURA has closed her eyes tightly and screwed up her face in concentration.)

LAURA.
I FEEL LIKE A MORON.
MICHAEL.
JUST TELL HIM THAT YOU'RE ON THE LINE.

(KLAPPER sighs, looks off in the distance, picks up her purse, and reluctantly starts off.)

MICHAEL.
COME ON, LAURA, CONCENTRATE!
LAURA. *(Concentrating furiously.)*
I FORGOT WHAT HE LOOKS LIKE!
MICHAEL.
WELL, LET'S SEE NOW,
HE'S SMALL AND HE'S JEWISH—

LAURA.
SHUT UP!
  MICHAEL.
PALLOR BLUISH.
  LAURA.
OKAY!!!
  MICHAEL.
KIND OF—
  LAURA.
WAIT, I CAN SEE HIM.
HE'S COMING!
I SEE HIM!
  MICHAEL AND LAURA.
OLE!
  LAURA.
MICHAEL, IT WORKED!
  MICHAEL.
I KNEW YOU'D GET THROUGH.
AND WASN'T IT FUN?
  LAURA.
WELL, YES.
  MICHAEL.
GOOD FOR YOU!
  MICHAEL AND LAURA.
SEE WHAT A LITTLE TEAMWORK CAN DO!

(After a final pause by the chessboard, KLAPPER is nearly off. REBECK runs on and almost knocks her over.)

REBECK. You!

(The MUSIC finishes in an irreverent cha-cha-cha.)

KLAPPER. It's nice to see you too, Rebeck. You look terrible. Sit awhile. Cool off.

(REBECK shoots MICHAEL and LAURA a look of reproach.)

LAURA. I didn't think you'd want to miss her.

REBECK. *(To LAURA, as KLAPPER hands him a tissue.)* Thanks.

KLAPPER. Don't mention it. So, Rebeck, you like it so much here, you're planning to move in?

REBECK. What do you mean?

KLAPPER. I mean a man your age should not go running in heat like this.

MICHAEL. You didn't want to miss her.

REBECK. I didn't want to miss you.

KLAPPER. *(After a moment, almost blushing with relief.)* Rebeck, what you lack in common sense, you make up in charm.

REBECK. *(Embarrassed, indicating Klapper's newspaper.)* A paper! I haven't seen one of these in ages.

KLAPPER. *(Handing it to him.)* They make them fresh every morning.

REBECK. Yes, but I … I never read them. Too depressing. *(And HE immediately buries himself in it.)*

KLAPPER. I know what you mean. I only get it for the funnies. The rest of it—trash. Nothing but wars and rapes and murders. I don't want to know from it.

REBECK. *(Barely listening.)* Mm.

MICHAEL. Don't be rude, Jonathan. You can read later.

(MICHAEL shakes his foot at REBECK, who swats at it, then covers by pretending to swat bugs. HE immediately re-buries himself in the paper.)

KLAPPER. You shouldn't leave your chessboard out like that. People will steal anything these days. Morris always left his out, but that was indoors. I've still got it just the way he left it. I think the black side is winning, but I guess we'll never know. So, Rebeck, what's so interesting there you don't want to hear an old lady talk about her dead husband?

(SHE peers over the shoulder of a still oblivious REBECK.)

KLAPPER. Professor Morgan and the shifty shiksa. You're right, Rebeck, that's a juicy one.

(At the sound of his name, both MICHAEL and LAURA react. THEY crowd over Rebeck's shoulder alongside KLAPPER. REBECK, suddenly aware, hastily shuts the paper.)

REBECK. Forgive me. I got distracted.
LAURA. What did it say?
KLAPPER. She's a cool customer, the wife.
MICHAEL. Who cares what it said?
KLAPPER. You think she did it?
REBECK. I wouldn't know. I only glanced at it.
LAURA. Don't you want to know?
MICHAEL. What for? I already know how it ends.
KLAPPER. The police think she did. And her lawyer wants her to cop a plea.
MICHAEL. What'd I tell you?
KLAPPER. But *she* says …
REBECK. How about a walk, Gertrude?
LAURA. Wait a minute.
KLAPPER. A walk?
LAURA. What *does* she say?
REBECK. We could visit Morris.
MICHAEL. Whatever it is, it's a lie.
KLAPPER. Why not? I'm sure he wouldn't mind. He'd like you.
MICHAEL. It's either lie or fry.
REBECK. *(Offering his arm.)* Shall we?
LAURA. She must have an excuse.
KLAPPER. *(Taking his arm.)* Thank you.

(THEY begin to exit.)

LAURA. What does she say?!
KLAPPER. But *she* says that *he* did it!
LAURA. What?
KLAPPER. That he committed suicide.

(LAURA and REBECK both look at MICHAEL.)

MICHAEL. I told you she'd lie.
KLAPPER. He had a book due his publisher that nobody can find. *She* says he hadn't even started it. She says he was written out. She says she told him she was leaving him and he snapped. Trouble is, she can't prove any of it.
REBECK. *(Helplessly furious.)* I thought you never read the papers!
KLAPPER. So I lied. Who knew you *were* interested in wars, rapes, and murders?
LAURA. And suicides.
MICHAEL. What's that crack supposed to mean?
REBECK. *(To LAURA and MICHAEL.)* I'm sorry.
KLAPPER. You and the rest of the world. *(SHE pats Rebeck's arm sympathetically. In so doing, SHE notices the absence of a watch on his wrist.)* So, I see you didn't find your watch, huh?

(And REBECK finally drags her off, shaking his head in frustration.)

LAURA. Well, congratulations.
MICHAEL. Now wait just a minute Laura.
LAURA. You really did it. You got me. You and your murdered man crying out for justice act.
MICHAEL. It's not an act!
LAURA. You used me!
MICHAEL. You can't believe Sandra.
LAURA. Jonathan believes her. You saw how he tried to get the widow out of here before she spilled the beans.

MICHAEL. You heard the beans. Nobody believes her. Not the papers, not the police. Hell, not even the church. They buried me with full rites in hallowed ground.

LAURA. Well, they'll just have to get out the shovels!

MICHAEL. You *want* to believe it.

LAURA. That's not true!

MICHAEL. It's what you've been looking for. An excuse. To check out.

LAURA. Better collect yourself, Michael. You're getting awfully fuzzy. In fact, you don't look at all like you anymore.

[Music Cue #11: WHAT DID YOU EXPECT INTRO]

(SHE dematerializes and runs downstage. MICHAEL calls after her.)

MICHAEL. Laura!

(As MUSIC begins, the LIGHTS go out, leaving harsh SPOTS on MICHAEL and LAURA, separated on opposite sides of the stage.)

Scene 6

(MICHAEL and LAURA are now in separate areas of the cemetery. THEY do not hear each other.)

LAURA. Liar!
MICHAEL. Laura!
LAURA. Liar!
MICHAEL. Laura! Damn!
JUST WHEN THINGS WERE GOING WELL.

LAURA.
I SHOULD HAVE KNOWN THAT THINGS WERE
GOING TOO WELL.
MICHAEL.
THERE WAS NO WAY SHE COULD TELL.
LAURA.
ONE LOOK AT HIM AND IT WAS EASY TO TELL.

LAURA.	**MICHAEL.**
EASY TO TELL!	HOW COULD SHE TELL?
EASY TO TELL!	HOW COULD SHE TELL?

BOTH.
I WONDER IF A GHOST CAN GO TO HELL?!
LAURA.
THERE IS NOTHING HE CAN SAY.
MICHAEL.
THERE MUST BE SOMETHING I CAN THINK OF
TO SAY.
LAURA.
I WON'T LISTEN IF HE DOES.
MICHAEL.
SHE'LL NEVER LISTEN—I DON'T CARE IF SHE
DOES!

LAURA.	**MICHAEL.**
AFTER TODAY,	ACTING THAT WAY,
WHY SHOULD I STAY?	ALL I CAN SAY—

BOTH.
I'D LIKE TO KNOW JUST WHO SHE/HE THINKS
SHE/HE WAS!
MICHAEL. Damn!

[Music Cue #12: WHAT DID YOU EXPECT/
LET ME EXPLAIN]

(LIGHTS out on MICHAEL.)

LAURA.
WHAT DID YOU EXPECT?
UNDERNEATH, YOU KNEW
THAT HE WAS MUCH TOO GOOD TO BE TRUE.
GALLANTRY'S AN EASY THING TO FAKE,
AND CHARM'S A PIECE OF CAKE,
YOU LET YOURSELF GET TAKEN LIKE YOU
  ALWAYS DO.
WHAT DID YOU EXPECT?
ANYONE COULD SEE
SOMETHING WAS AWRY,
BUT YOU WERE MUCH TOO READY TO BUY.
ALL HE HAD TO DO WAS PUFF HIS CHEST
AND YOU WERE SO IMPRESSED.
A HALF-WIT COULD HAVE GUESSED THAT IT
  WAS ALL A LIE!
WHAT DID YOU EXPECT?
SAY GOODNIGHT AND CLOSE YOUR EYES.
MAKE YOUR PEACE AND YOUR GOODBYES.
END THE ENDLESS LIES.
WHAT MORE CAN YOU EXPECT?

*(LIGHTS out on LAURA and up on MICHAEL,
  pacing.)*

MICHAEL.
LAURA, LET ME EXPLAIN.
I DIDN'T MEAN TO DO IT.
SO, EVEN THOUGH I DID,
IT'S NOT A LIE
TO SAY THE THINGS I SAID.
I ONLY SAID
I DIDN'T *WANT* TO DIE.
WHY DO YOU THINK
I DOCTORED UP THE STORY?
YOU WOULDN'T UNDERSTAND,

I DIDN'T *WANT* TO DIE.
I TOLD YOU THE TRUTH.
I ALTERED THE FACTS,
BUT I TOLD YOU THE TRUTH!
I'VE GOT TO EXPLAIN.
SANDRA DROVE ME TO IT.
SHE SAID THAT WE WERE THROUGH.
I WAS A WRECK
AND SHE WAS CHECKING OUT.
WHAT COULD I DO?
I WANTED HER TO PAY.
I ONLY KNEW
THAT WHEN THE CHIPS WERE FALLING,
THE LADY WALKED AWAY.
I WANTED HER TO PAY!
A CHILD COULD SEE
I WAS STRIKING AT *HER*
AT *HER* NOT AT *ME*.
AT *HER* NOT AT *ME*!
DON'T YOU SEE?
DON'T YOU SEE?!
NO, YOU DON'T.
WELL, YOU COULD,
BUT YOU WON'T!

*(HE pauses in frustration, visibly trying to calm himself.
    HE strikes a pleading tone.)*

LAURA, LOOK AT ME.
OPEN YOUR EYES.
LOOK AT THE LIFE
STILL INSIDE ME.
IF I REALLY HAD *WANTED* TO DIE,
HOW COULD I STAY?
WHY WOULD I TRY?
LAURA, STAY WITH ME.
I'M IN YOUR HANDS.
YOU ARE THE LIFE

SHE DENIED ME.
IF I HADN'T BEEN WILLING TO LIE,
YOU WOULDN'T BE HERE.
AND NEITHER WOULD I.

(LIGHTS out on MICHAEL and up on LAURA.)

LAURA.
HE SAID HE NEEDED ME.
WHAT A THING TO SAY.
HE DOESN'T REALLY CARE ABOUT *ME*.
IF ONLY HE COULD CARE ABOUT *ME*,
I'D HAPPILY—
THAT'S ENOUGH OF THAT!
TIME FOR YOU TO GO.
REGRETS ARE MUCH TOO EASY TO GROW.
ONCE YOU ENTERTAIN A RAY OF HOPE,
YOU'RE STRINGING UP A ROPE.
PANDORA'S BOX IS OPENING AND YOU WELL
  KNOW
WHAT YOU CAN EXPECT!

(LIGHTS on BOTH now.)

LAURA.	**MICHAEL.**
CLOSE YOUR EYES!	ALL RIGHT, SO I LIED!
FORGET THE MAN.	IF YOU HAD REALLY
	MET THE MAN
WE WERE THROUGH	MET THE MAN I
WHEN WE BEGAN.	KNEW,
RUN WHILE YOU	THEN WE WOULD
STILL CAN.	BOTH BE THROUGH.
	LAURA, WHAT ELSE
	COULD I DO?
YOU'VE GOT TO	
CLOSE YOUR EYES.	
WHY CAN'T I CLOSE	
MY EYES!?	

STOP ACTING LIKE A
  FOOL.
HE ISN'T SUCH A
  PRIZE.
HE DOESN'T EVEN
CARE ABOUT YOU,
BUT HE'S NOT THE
  ONE
TELLING LIES.

LAURA, ONLY ONE
THING IS TRUE.
I LOVE YOU.
I WAS A FOOL.

I DIDN'T KNOW

HOW I
CARED ABOUT YOU.

IF YOU KNEW THE
  TRUTH
YOU WOULD GO.
I CAN'T LET YOU GO!

EACH TIME I CLOSE
  MY EYES,
HE'S ALL I'M
  THINKING OF.
OH, WHAT A TIME
TO FIN'LLY FALL IN
  LOVE.
IN LOVE!

*(LIGHTS out on THEM and up on KLAPPER and
  REBECK in another section of the cemetery.)*

KLAPPER. I know she's around here somewhere.
Esther was Morris's favorite aunt. After she died, we
used to visit her every year for her birthday. This year I
got lost. It's such a small stone. And it was Morris who
knew the way.

REBECK. I've never noticed another Klapper
anywhere.

KLAPPER. It's not Klapper. It's Kravitz.

REBECK. Kravitz? You mean Esther Kravitz?

KLAPPER. You knew *her*?

REBECK. No! But I know where she is. Right off the corner of Laurel Avenue and Linden Lane. It's a lovely grave. Impeccably kept. And she's got a beautiful little Star of David. I'll show you the way.

(HE starts off. KLAPPER remains.)

KLAPPER. You got the time?
REBECK. Sure. I'm not doing anything.
KLAPPER. No, I mean the time. On your watch.
REBECK. (*Involuntarily hides his empty wrist.*) I told you. I forgot it today. I'm always forgetting things.
KLAPPER. Sure, I know. Watches, chessboards. So how come you're so good at gravestones? (*Pause.*) [Music Cue #13: IT'S NONE OF MY BUSINESS] Forgive me. I shouldn't play detective.
IT'S NONE OF MY BUSINESS.
FORGET WHAT I SAID.
I ASK TOO MANY QUESTIONS.
  REBECK. No—
  KLAPPER.
YES.
IT'S NONE OF MY BUSINESS,
SO GO RIGHT AHEAD,
GO—MAKE MY EARS BURN.
  REBECK. Gertrude—
  KLAPPER.
IT SEEMS THAT I NEVER
KNOW WHEN TO SAY WHEN.
MY QUESTION'S NOT ANSWERED,
I ASK IT AGAIN
WHEN
IT'S NONE OF MY BUSINESS.
YOU'D THINK ALREADY I'D LEARN.
  REBECK. Gertrude, about the watch—
  KLAPPER. What watch?
IT'S NONE OF MY BUSINESS
YOU TOLD ME A LIE.

SURELY YOU HAD YOUR REASONS.

(HE opens his mouth to reply.)

PLEASE!
IT'S NONE OF MY BUSINESS.
I WOULDN'T ASK WHY.
I DON'T WANT TO KNOW.
BELIEVE ME, I'M SORRY
I CAUGHT YOU THAT WAY.
IF MORRIS WERE HERE
I KNOW JUST WHAT HE'D SAY:
HE'D SAY, "MIND YOUR OWN BUSINESS."
IT'S NEVER MY BUSINESS.
I THINK MAYBE I SHOULD GO.
   So?

(There is an awkward silence. REBECK sits as if immobilized. MICHAEL's voice drifts into the silence. A QUARTET begins.)

MICHAEL.	REBECK.	LAURA.	KLAPPER.

LAURA, I
  CAN'T
TELL YOU
  THE
TRUTH. YOU
  DON'T
WANT THE
  TRUTH.
SO TO HELL
  WITH
THE TRUTH!			

		HE SAID HE NEEDED ME. WHAT IF IT'S THE TRUTH?	

WHAT IF
EV'RY–
THING HE
SAID
IS THE
TRUTH?

NOW IS THE
HOUR
AND HERE
IS THE
PLACE TO
GATHER
YOUR
NERVE
AND
FACE UP TO
THE
FACE—I
WONDER
IF I COULD
EXPLAIN? I
KNOW

I KNOW I   I REALLY
SHOULD   SHOULD
EXPLAIN.   EXPLAIN.
BUT I   NO, I
CAN'T   CAN'T
POSSIBLY   POSSIBLY
EXPLAIN.   EXPLAIN.

NOW, YOUR
EYES
ARE WIDE.
SHOW HIM
WHAT'S
INSIDE.
YOU'VE GOT
TO
TELL HIM   JUST TELL
SO.   HIM
                  YOU'RE
                  SORRY

			JUST TELL HIM AND GO. YOU ASK TOO MANY QUESTIONS.
	AH, BUT IF I TELL A LIE,	LET HIM KNOW.	
LAURA, I ONLY KNOW		GO AHEAD AND DROP THE POSE,	IT'S NONE OF YOUR BUSINESS HE TOLD YOU A LIE.
I CAN'T LET YOU GO.	THEN, I HAVE TO SAY GOODBYE.	SHOW	IT'S NONE OF YOUR BUSINESS, I'VE GOT TO KNOW
HOW WILL I EVER SEE SHE	CAN I POSSIBLY EXPLAIN?	HIM NOW, AND ONCE IT SHOWS,	WHY! JUST HOW BAD CAN IT BE?
NEVER	WHO	ONCE HE REALLY	GOD

KNOWS
WHO
  KNOWS
WHO
  KNOWS?
	KNOWS?
	WHO
	  KNOWS?
	WHO
	  KNOWS?
		KNOWS–
		WHO
		  KNOWS?
		WHO
		  KNOWS?
			KNOWS!
			WHO
			  KNOWS?
			WHO
			  KNOWS?

MICHAEL. What the hell am I going to tell her?

LAURA. I've got to tell him!

KLAPPER. So long, Rebeck.

REBECK. Gertrude! Sit down.

(An attentive KLAPPER sits on the steps of a convenient mausoleum. As SHE fixes REBECK with a

questioning stare, there is a final CHORD in the orchestra.)

End of ACT I

ACT II

[Music Cue #14: OPENING ACT II]
[Music Cue #15: WHAT SHOULD I DO?]

Scene 1

(The curtain rises. KLAPPER is sitting in front of Morris's mausoleum in a downstage corner. REBECK is sitting in front of his mausoleum, with the RAVEN perched upon it, in the opposite corner. HE is eating a sandwich. MICHAEL and LAURA are upstage center, sitting on the cemetery wall overlooking the city. The characters are revealed by LIGHT as their turn to speak arrives.)

KLAPPER. I couldn't believe it either, Morris. Right here in the cemetery. The man is your neighbor. Not that he's hurting anybody, I suppose. I said I wouldn't turn him in. But somebody's got to help him.

(Switch to REBECK and the RAVEN.)

REBECK. What else could I do?
RAVEN. Lie.
REBECK. I'd never see her again.
RAVEN. True.
REBECK. She promised she wouldn't tell.
RAVEN. Sure.
REBECK. *(Bites into the sandwich. HE sputters.)* Ugh. What's wrong with this pickle?
RAVEN. It's kosher.

(Switch to LAURA and MICHAEL.)

LAURA. I don't know what came over me.
MICHAEL. It doesn't matter.
LAURA. I knew you couldn't have killed yourself. Not you.
MICHAEL. It's finished. Forgotten.
LAURA. Forgiven?
MICHAEL. Of course. *(HE squints at her.)* You're a bit wavy today. Is that a new dress?
LAURA. I had to imagine it. I never had one like it before. Is it all right?

(Switch to KLAPPER. SHE sings.)

    KLAPPER.
I'LL STAY AWAY.
MORRIS, I PROMISE, NO
"IFS," "ANDS," OR "BUTS."
HE COULD BE NUTS.
I COULD MEET A TERRIBLE END.
BUT, THEN, AGAIN,
MORRIS, HE TRUSTED ME,
TOLD ME THE TRUTH.
THAT ISN'T NUTS.
MAYBE ALL HE NEEDS IS A FRIEND.
    LAURA.
TELL HIM.
STOP THIS ABSURD HESITATION.
WHOEVER CAPTURED THE PRINCE
DROPPING HINTS?
JUST TELL HIM.
AND IF THE MAN DOESN'T SHARE IT,
SOMEHOW OR OTHER, YOU'LL BEAR IT.
    KLAPPER AND LAURA.
WHAT SHOULD I DO?
OH, YES, IT'S EASY TO AGREE
TO FOLLOW YOUR HEART,
BUT IT'S MUCH HARDER

DIGGING UP THE COURAGE TO START.
DANGEROUS, TOO.
WHAT SHOULD I DO?

(Switch to REBECK and the RAVEN.)

REBECK. How long has it been?
RAVEN. Almost a week.
REBECK. She needs time.
RAVEN. Uh-huh. Bellevue's got a waiting list.

(Switch to KLAPPER.)

KLAPPER. I know, I know, he lives in a cemetery, he's got to be crazy. Well, I'm here a lot too, Morris. So what does that make me?

(Switch to MICHAEL and LAURA.)

LAURA. Remember the day we met?
MICHAEL. Yes?
LAURA. I told you I wanted to go to sleep?
MICHAEL. Yes?
LAURA. I lied.

(Switch to REBECK.)

REBECK.
WHAT THE HELL IS GOING ON WITH HER?
SEVEN DAYS AND STILL SHE'S GONE,
WITH HER CONVENTIONALITY IN TOW.
SHOULD I BE STAYING HERE OR LAYING LOW?
I NEVER SHOULD HAVE SAID A WORD TO HER.
THE TRUTH WOULD NEVER HAVE OCCURRED TO
  HER.
BUT, NO, I HAD TO PRESS MY LUCK,
AND NOW I'M STUCK HERE LIKE A SITTING
  DUCK.

MICHAEL.
MORGAN, YOU BETTER FACE IT KID,
THE LADY'S IN LOVE WITH YOU.
TOO BAD THERE'S NO WAY FOR YOU TO TELL
  HER
THAT YOU'RE FEELING THE SAME WAY, TOO.
NOT WHEN THE FELLA THE LADY FELL FOR
IS A FELLA YOU NEVER EVEN KNEW.
REBECK AND MICHAEL.
WHAT SHOULD I DO?
MY NERVES ARE SLOWLY TURNING
INTO YESTERDAY'S HASH,
SITTING HERE WAITING FOR
THE OTHER SHOE TO GO SMASH.
I NEED A CLUE.
WHAT SHOULD I DO?
KLAPPER.
HE'S NOT A NUT,
AND, MORRIS, HE NEEDS ME!
IS THAT SUCH A CRIME?
MORRIS, IT'S TIME,
THAT I—
LAURA.
TELL HIM.
THERE'S ONLY ONE WAY TO PLAY IT,
OPEN YOUR MOUTH AND JUST SAY IT!
REBECK.
I NEVER SHOULD HAVE SAID A WORD TO HER.
THE TRUTH WOULD NEVER HAVE OCCURRED TO
  HER.
BUT NOW I'VE SHOCKED HER TO THE CORE,
AND I MIGHT NEVER SEE HER ANY—
MICHAEL.
MORGAN, YOU BETTER HOPE AND PRAY
THAT LOVE REALLY CAN BE BLIND.
BECAUSE THE FELLA THE LADY FELL FOR
AIN'T THE FELLA THE LADY'S GONNA FIND!

ALL FOUR.
WHAT SHOULD I DO?
IF I COULD ONLY KNOW
EXACTLY WHAT WOULD COME TRUE,
I'D HAVE NO TROUBLE
MAKING UP MY MIND WHAT TO DO.
LAURA.
DOES HE LOVE ME?
KLAPPER.
HE TRUSTED ME.
MICHAEL.
SHE'S NOT IN LOVE WITH *ME*.
REBECK.
WHERE CAN SHE BE?
LAURA.
AND WHAT SHOULD I...
KLAPPER.
AND WHAT SHOULD I...
MICHAEL.
AND WHAT SHOULD I...
REBECK.
AND WHAT SHOULD I...
ALL FOUR.
DO? WHAT SHOULD I DO?

(The LIGHTS fade on MICHAEL and LAURA. KLAPPER crosses to REBECK.)

Scene 2

KLAPPER. Ida would have me locked up if she knew I came back here.

REBECK. You told her about me?!

KLAPPER. I may be crazy, but I'm not stupid. It's the police I'd tell. Or that gatekeeper. The one that makes you "nervous."

REBECK. But you didn't?

KLAPPER. What good would it do? They'd just kick you out. Into the gutter. You wouldn't last in the gutter, Rebeck. Trust me.

REBECK. I'm glad you came back.

KLAPPER. I had to visit Morris.

REBECK. Maybe you'll come again?

KLAPPER. Rebeck, this is no life for a man. I have this apartment. Huge.

REBECK. No, Gertrude. I couldn't.

KLAPPER. You could rent. After you get a job.

REBECK. I don't mean to sound ungrateful—

KLAPPER. So don't.

REBECK. It isn't possible.

KLAPPER. You worried about the neighbors, maybe? So they talk. I'm a widow. I got a right to have boarders.

REBECK. You don't understand, Gertrude. I don't live here because I have to. I prefer it here.

KLAPPER. C'mon, Rebeck, you're not some crazy doesn't have enough sense to come in out of the snow. Don't be so proud. It's no shame to go broke. Ask Iaccocca.

REBECK. I didn't go broke. I like it here.

KLAPPER. For God's sake, let me *do* something for you.

(There is a MUSICAL PLOP. KLAPPER claps her hand to her hat, then removes and examines it.)

REBECK. What is it?

KLAPPER. Some bird's got terrific aim.

(The LIGHTS fade on KLAPPER and REBECK and come up on MICHAEL and LAURA at the cemetery wall.)

LAURA. Did I say it wrong, Michael? I wouldn't be surprised. I haven't had very much practice.
MICHAEL. You said it beautifully.
LAURA. I must have loved you from the start. Why else would I have been so awful to you?
MICHAEL. I don't know. Good taste?

(Pause. LAURA looks away from him at the city.)

LAURA. I'm glad we came here tonight. The city is so alive. I never noticed it before. Let's come here often.
MICHAEL. Laura, I'm a bit overwhelmed. And I'm not really sure of what to say.
LAURA. Whatever you feel.
MICHAEL. I feel it's a mistake. We're ghosts, Laura. How can we love? Spiritually? That isn't enough.
LAURA. I'll take whatever I can get.
MICHAEL. You can't even take my hand. It's ludicrous. We could never really know each other. Never be truly intimate.
LAURA. Yes, we could. We could know each other completely. More completely than we ever could have when we were alive.
MICHAEL. (*Afraid of what's coming.*) What do you mean?
LAURA. You know. (*SHE taps her head, echoing the same gesture and line in THE TELEPATHETIQUE.*) You taught me. We could know everything.
MICHAEL. That would be very foolish.
LAURA. Not if we love each other.
MICHAEL. People live whole lifetimes without knowing themselves, much less each other. There's a good reason for that.
LAURA. We don't have a lifetime. All we have for sure is now.
MICHAEL. There's too much you don't know about me.

LAURA. I know that I love you. Nothing could change that.

MICHAEL. Something could.

LAURA. What?

MICHAEL. I don't love you. I can't love you. I'm sorry, Laura. I wish I didn't have to say it.

LAURA. This wasn't supposed to happen.

MICHAEL. If there were any other way …

LAURA. It's all wrong.

MICHAEL. Let's not talk about it anymore.

LAURA. Just go, Michael. Please. Just go.

(HE looks at her for a moment then exits. [Music Cue #16: CLOSE YOUR EYES] SHE turns to look only after HE has disappeared.)

LAURA.
CLOSE YOUR EYES.
CLOSE YOUR EYES.
LIFE IS AT AN END.
JUST LET IT GO.
THERE IS NOTHING MORE YOU NEED TO KNOW.
IT'S OVER.
CLOSE YOUR EYES.
CLOSE YOUR EYES.
NOW THAT EV'RY HOPE IS BLOWN APART,
TIME THAT YOU WERE KINDER TO YOUR HEART.
ALL YOUR LIFE
YOU SHUT THE DOOR.
SO AFRAID OF WANTING MORE.
NOW, YOU KNOW WHAT FOR.
FAIR WARNING.
CLOSE YOUR EYES.
CLOSE YOUR EYES.
BE GLAD YOU FOUND THE NERVE TO TRY.
IT'S YOU WHO SAID HE SHOULDN'T LIE.
ALL YOUR LIFE
YOU LONGED TO KNOW,

KNOW IF LOVE WAS EVER SO.
NOW YOU KNOW.
CLOSE YOUR EYES.
CLOSE YOUR EYES.

(The LIGHTS fade.)

[Music Cue #16a: THE MORRIS WALTZ]

Scene 3

(REBECK enters from inside the mausoleum. HE is plugged in to a Walkman, which peeks out of his pocket. His clothes are new and HE carries a thermos and a matching chess set on top of a frilly pillow, which HE drops on the mausoleum steps. The RAVEN enters, flies to the mausoleum and, just before REBECK is to sit on the pillow, steals it, dropping it over the cemetery wall. With a sigh, REBECK takes off the earphones. The RAVEN flies to him and lets out a loud squawk right in his ear. REBECK jumps.)

REBECK. What was that for?
RAVEN. Just testing.
REBECK. *(Removing the tape from the player.)* I don't know. I still think *Les Miserables* was meant to be read. Morris loved it. It's the last show he and Gertrude saw.
RAVEN. What's next, his truss?
REBECK. Don't be snide. It makes her feel useful.
RAVEN. Whatever you say.
REBECK. She's late.
RAVEN. Maybe Morris got jealous.
REBECK. They lock the gates at five. We won't have much time.

(Suddenly, we hear KLAPPER's voice.)

KLAPPER. *(Off.)* Hey! Rebeck!

(REBECK scrambles up, fussing nervously with his rumpled appearance. The RAVEN spreads his wings in preparation for flight.)

REBECK. You always leave. You don't have to, you know.
RAVEN. I just ate.

(And HE's off. KLAPPER enters, wearing an absurd, crescent-shaped hat.)

KLAPPER. Rebeck, sorry I'm late. There was this train in front and this train behind and a big tsimmis with the whistle.

(REBECK is staring at her hat.)

KLAPPER. Alright, already. It's just a hat. You want I should wear a pith helmet like Dr. Livingstone?
REBECK. How on earth does it stay on?
KLAPPER. I had this jar of library paste, it seemed a shame to waste it. Leave the hat, Rebeck, it never hurt you.
REBECK. I waited all afternoon. I thought you weren't coming.
KLAPPER. It's good you should worry a little. Keeps you from getting fat. *(SHE flops down on the mausoleum steps like they were a sofa. The shoes come off.)* Completely numb. My toes got no more feeling than a salted herring.
REBECK. You ought to wear sneakers.
KLAPPER. What am I, a cheerleader? What would Morris think if I showed up in sneakers? Sometimes you worry me, Rebeck.
REBECK. You don't have to worry about me.

KLAPPER. I brought you something. *(SHE begins rummaging in her purse.)*

REBECK. Gertrude! You promised.

KLAPPER. I know, I know. I couldn't help it. This place is such a dump. It's falling down. I wake up nights and I think what happens when the roof caves in? Even your thick skull couldn't take that.

REBECK. I promise you, it's safe. And if it ever becomes a problem, I'll just move.

KLAPPER. That was my idea.

REBECK. I meant to another mausoleum.

KLAPPER. So did I.

REBECK. You did?

KLAPPER. I had a set of keys made.

REBECK. Keys?

KLAPPER. To Morris's house.

REBECK. You're not serious.

KLAPPER. Why not? You won't come live in mine.

REBECK. I couldn't possibly.

KLAPPER. Don't be such a baby. Morris has everything. Even heat.

REBECK. You heated his grave?

KLAPPER. I should only visit when it's warm? Of course I heated it. It's also roomy, sturdy, and clean. And planted. Morris is always in bloom. Aha! *(SHE triumphantly extracts the keys from her bag.)*

REBECK. You're crazy.

KLAPPER. *(Holding them out to him.)* You feel funny, you think he'd mind? Morris won't mind. Take my word on it.

REBECK. This has gone far enough.

KLAPPER. It's just a house. *(SHE shakes the keys at him.)* Here.

REBECK. It's Morris's house!!

[Music Cue #17: ARGUMENT]

*(HE knocks the keys out of her outstretched hand,
    startling them both. There is a moment of shocked
    silence, then:)*

 REBECK.
I HAVE MORRIS'S CLOTHES,
I HAVE MORRIS'S WATCH,
EVEN MORRIS'S CHESS SET,
 KLAPPER. His *extra* set.
 REBECK.
AND NOW I'M EXPECTED TO MOVE
INTO MORRIS'S GRAVE!
WELL, IT'S OVER NOW.
GERTRUDE, IT'S OVER AND DONE.
FROM NOW ON I'M THROUGH
BEING MORRIS FOR YOU.
 KLAPPER. Who asked you to?
 REBECK.
THE FIRST TIME YOU SAW ME,
YOU THOUGHT I WAS MORRIS'S GHOST.
AND OVER AND OVER I HEAR
HOW I SHARE HIS APPEAL.
HE WAS ALWAYS
THE SWEETEST, THE SMARTEST, THE FINEST,
  THE MOST.
THE *MOST* IMPOSSIBLE,
MOST UNBEARABLE,
MOST UNREAL!
 KLAPPER. What would you know about it?
 REBECK.
STOP KIDDING YOURSELF.
THERE'S NOT A CHANCE HE WAS HALF
WHAT YOU SAY.
YOU'RE KIDDING YOURSELF
WHEN YOU RECALL HIM THAT WAY.
THIS IMAGE YOU PAINT,
YOU ONLY CONTRIVE.
HE WASN'T A SAINT

AND HE ISN'T ALIVE.
STOP KIDDING YOURSELF!
    KLAPPER. Kidding myself?! Look who's talking.
TAKE A LOOK AT YOURSELF,
LIVING WITH DEAD ONES
AND HIDING FROM PEOPLE.
    REBECK. This is *not* about me.
    KLAPPER.
I'LL TELL YOU WHAT KIND OF A LIFE
YOU'VE BEEN LIVING IN HERE:
LIKE AN ANIMAL,
HUNTED AND CRAZY AND SAD.
FROM NOW ON I'M THROUGH
PLAYING NURSEMAID FOR YOU.
    REBECK. That's fine with me.
    KLAPPER.
SO MY MEM'RIES ARE COCKEYED,
PLEASE TELL ME, JUST WHO DOES IT HURT?
WHY SHOULD I REMEMBER HOW
MADDENING MORRIS COULD BE?
BUT A MAN LIKES TO LIVE IN A GRAVE,
I'LL TELL *YOU* WHO IT HURTS:
IT HURTS HIMSELF AND
IT HURTS HIS FRIENDS AND
IT'S HURTING *ME*!
    REBECK. It's got nothing to do with you.
    KLAPPER.
STOP KIDDING YOURSELF.
COME OUT AND LIVE IN THE WORLD
LIKE A MAN. YOU'RE KIDDING YOURSELF
IF YOU DON'T THINK THAT YOU CAN.
I JUST WANT TO SEE
THE BEST THING FOR YOU—
    REBECK.
WHICH JUST HAPPENS TO BE
WHAT'S THE BEST THING FOR *YOU*!
    BOTH.
STOP KIDDING YOURSELF!

KLAPPER. What *is* it with you?! Huh?! Look, Rebeck, whatever reason you think you got to be here, it's not good enough. There's a million stories in the naked city. Businesses go bust, teenagers get acne, husbands die. But people survive. They go on. And not by running off to live at Forest Lawn.
REBECK. You're right, Gertrude. Some of them just visit a lot.
KLAPPER. You *are* just like Morris! Stubborn and willful and all dried up ... *(SHE stops herself as SHE realizes what's coming out. SHE scrambles for her things.)* I don't care what you do. Bury yourself in your crazy world. But don't look for me. You want me, take yourself a ride on the goddamn IRT. *(SHE points at the keys lying on the ground.)* You better keep those. It's gonna be a cold winter.

(And SHE exits. REBECK cannot watch her receding figure. HE reaches down, picks up the keys and exits into the mausoleum as the MUSIC finishes quietly. The LIGHTS provide us with yet another transformation to morning. It is the next day.)

Scene 4

(The RAVEN enters and drops a bag from Bagel Nosh on the mausoleum steps. HE spies Klapper's thermos and, after checking to see if REBECK is about, picks it up and drops it over the cemetery wall, where it CRASHES loudly. REBECK comes out in a bathrobe and slippers. HE extracts a bagel from the bag and stares at it.)

RAVEN. Just pretend it's ham and cheese on white.
REBECK. You're skating on thin ice, bird.
RAVEN. Touchy. Touchy.

LAURA. (*Enters.*) Hello, Jonathan. I've come to say goodbye.
RAVEN. Well, well. Two for the price of one.
LAURA. What?
REBECK. It's Gertrude. She won't be coming back.
RAVEN. Nevermore.
LAURA. Well, I'm leaving too. I'm going off to sit quietly by myself and stay far away from anything that might keep me up a second longer than necessary.
REBECK. But what about Michael?
LAURA. He'll manage.
REBECK. What happened?
LAURA. Nothing. Quite literally.
REBECK. You're wrong, Laura. The two of you have the impossible. I know, because I've never seen it here before. Don't be so quick to give it up.
LAURA. I thought your job was to help us accept death.
REBECK. So did I.
RAVEN. Better beat it, kid. Lazarus is on the march.
REBECK. Stay and talk to him.
LAURA. No. I've been humiliated enough for one death.

[Music Cue # 17a: DISAPPEARANCE CUES]

(*And SHE dematerializes. SHE stays to watch, however, as MICHAEL enters.*)

MICHAEL. Jonathan. I've come to say goodbye.
RAVEN. Gin.
REBECK. This is ridiculous.
MICHAEL. I'm going to miss you too.
REBECK. What have the two of you done to each other?
MICHAEL. Didn't she tell you?
REBECK. No.
MICHAEL. Then neither will I.

RAVEN. *(With a loud squawk.)* Just when I thought it was safe to come back to the cemetery!
REBECK. What is it now?
RAVEN. Just remember, Rebeck. Her noodle pudding's already killed once.

(The RAVEN exits abruptly as KLAPPER bustles on. SHE is dressed casually, rather than respectfully, and is sporting a pair of pink sneakers on her feet.)

REBECK. Gertrude! *(HE gathers the robe about him in embarrassment.)* How did you get in? The gate's not even open yet.
KLAPPER. Fidel lost a little beauty sleep.

(REBECK notices her sneakers.)

KLAPPER. O.K. So they're pink. White shows the dirt.
REBECK. Are you all right?
KLAPPER. I been up all night, Rebeck. And I did a lot of thinking. I got no business telling you how to live your life. And you got no business telling me how to live mine. Even if we *were* right. I'm sorry I yelled at you. And I hope you'll be okay here. But you won't be seeing me anymore. It's time that Morris got what he came for—a little rest.
REBECK. Don't stop visiting Morris just because of me, Gertrude. I'll keep out of your way. I'm an expert at it.
KLAPPER. I got things to do. After sixty years, it's time that Gertrude Klapper and I spent some time together. We hardly know each other.
REBECK. I don't understand.
KLAPPER. I've worn out my welcome here, Rebeck. And so have you.
REBECK. Don't start that again.

KLAPPER. All right, all right. Honestly. Next to you, Morris was Neville Chamberlain. So goodbye. You're a good man, Jonathan. A little meshuga, but a good man. *(SHE starts off, then turns.)* You still got my number?

(REBECK nods. SHE turns back.)

REBECK. Gertrude. Wait.
KLAPPER. *(Almost too eagerly.)* What?
REBECK. There's something I've got to tell you.
KLAPPER. You mean there's more? What'd you do, Rebeck, vote for Nixon?
REBECK. You've got to know the real reason why I can't go with you.
MICHAEL. Don't, Jonathan.
KLAPPER. You mean you've got one?
MICHAEL. She'll call the men in the white coats.
REBECK. I won't have you thinking it's because of you.
KLAPPER. So what should I think?
REBECK. I can't leave because, because I have this gift. It's very special, nobody else has it, and—oh what's the point?
KLAPPER. I don't know, Rebeck. Maybe you should come to it.
MICHAEL. She'll destroy you, Jonathan.
REBECK. You'll never believe me.
LAURA. *(Rematerializes.)* Give her a chance.

(MICHAEL stares at LAURA in surprise. SHE returns his gaze steadily.)

KLAPPER. Rebeck!
REBECK. *(Staring at LAURA in surprise.)* I talk to ghosts.
KLAPPER. Is that all?

REBECK. Ghosts, Gertrude. Of the people they bury here.

KLAPPER. A week outside and you'll forget all about it.

REBECK. You don't understand. I'm all they have. Nobody else can see them. Nobody else can help them. They need me. It's what I do. That's why I can't leave. It's not because I wouldn't like to. It's not because of you.

KLAPPER. It's all right, Rebeck. You don't have to explain. But if I were you, I'd lay off the Shirley MacLaine books. *(SHE turns as if to go.)*

REBECK. *(Reaching forward and grasping both her hands.)* You must believe me.

MICHAEL. Jonathan!

LAURA. *(To MICHAEL.)* Leave him alone!

REBECK. *(In absolute fury.)* Will you stop it?!

KLAPPER. *(With a touch of real fear.)* What did I do?

REBECK. Not you, Gertrude. Them.

KLAPPER. Them?

REBECK. There are two of them here right now. And they're the most frustrating, annoying, hopeless pair I've ever had to deal with.

KLAPPER. *Two* of them?

REBECK. Something impossible has happened between them. Something I've never seen in all my time here.

KLAPPER. What's that?

REBECK. Love.

[Music Cue #18: NO ONE EVER KNOWS]

(KLAPPER's hand goes to her mouth. SHE starts to tremble with excitement SHE is trying to hide.)

REBECK. It's a miracle and they're both about to walk away from it. And I don't know what to say to them.

KLAPPER. So what's to say?
TELL "THEM" TO PLAY OR PASS.
TELL "THEM" TO BID OR FOLD.
TELL "THEM" LOVERS OUGHT TO HAVE THE
  COMMON SENSE
TO COME IN FROM THE COLD.

REBECK. Would you? Talk to them? You and Morris had thirty years together. Maybe they'd listen to you.

KLAPPER. "They" haven't listened yet.

REBECK. They need reassurance.

KLAPPER. If you want guarantees, you don't fall in love, you buy IBM.

REBECK. Help them.

(KLAPPER looks at REBECK helplessly. Then, SHE gives in and addresses "them," rather than him. Throughout the song, SHE keeps turning back to REBECK, until, finally, SHE abandons all subterfuge of the ghosts.)

KLAPPER. I'm sorry.
I CAN'T SAY THE THINGS
THAT YOU WANT TO HEAR,
FOR, THE TRUTH IS,
LOVE DOESN'T ALWAYS CARRY YOU OVER
  FEAR.
THE BRAVEST HEARTS WIND UP
IN PIECES.
NO ONE EVER KNOWS.
YOU CAN THINK YOU'RE SAFE,
SAFE AS YOU CAN BE.
ALL IT REALLY MEANS IS
YOU ONLY SEE WHAT YOU WANT TO SEE.
IT ALL CAN FALL APART

AT RANDOM.
NO ONE EVER KNOWS.
PEOPLE HURT EACH OTHER.
CHILDREN KNOW IT'S TRUE.
BUT THERE'S NO ONE ELSE CAN HURT YOU
HALF AS MUCH AS YOU.
BUILD YOURSELF A FORTRESS
AND YOU MAY SURVIVE,
BUT WHEN YOU'VE LOCKED EV'RYONE OUT,
THEN WHO'S GONNA CARE YOU'RE ALIVE?
TAKE A STEP OUTSIDE
AND YOU COULD BE THROUGH.
ON THE OTHER HAND,
YOU COULD FIND IT ISN'T SO HARD TO DO.
YOU HAVE TO LEARN TO RISK THE JOURNEY.
DON'T GET CRAZY WHERE IT GOES.
NO ONE EVER KNOWS.

(SHE reaches out her hand to REBECK. HE reaches for it, but can't take it and exits abruptly into the mausoleum. KLAPPER is crushed.)

LAURA. *(Also crushed.)* Jonathan.

(KLAPPER struggles to keep her composure.)

    KLAPPER.
TAKE A STEP OUTSIDE.
YOU CAN MAKE IT THROUGH.
SO, ALL RIGHT, YOU'LL GO IT ALONE,
IT CAN'T BE SO HARD TO DO.
YOU HAVE TO LEARN TO RISK
THE JOURNEY.

(The MELODY finishes as SHE gives a last look after REBECK, then squares her shoulders, takes a deep breath and exits. MICHAEL and LAURA watch sadly.

As MICHAEL turns to look at LAURA, SHE turns away from him.)

MICHAEL. I thought I'd lost you.
LAURA. I hadn't meant to be found.
MICHAEL. There's something you should know. You don't love me.
LAURA. That's a relief.
MICHAEL. I'm not heroic. Or gallant. Or defiant. Just scared. I was a lousy writer. But I couldn't face it. And I wasn't murdered. Everything I said was a lie. Including "I don't love you."
LAURA. That's enough.
MICHAEL. You fell in love with a lie.
LAURA. Stop it!
MICHAEL. Laura, I've spent my whole life trying to be what other people wanted me to be. A writer instead of a teacher. A genius instead of a son. Hemingway instead of a husband. I thought you wanted a hero. Nobody ever wanted *me* before. How was I supposed to know?
LAURA. If we had met while we were alive, you'd never have looked at me twice.
MICHAEL. You'd never have let me. (*Stung, SHE turns to look at him.*) [Music Cue #19: BECAUSE OF THEM ALL] It's time we both had a good look. Just like you wanted.
I HAVE SO MUCH IN ME
I HAVE TRIED TO CONCEAL:
ALL THE HATREDS AND HYPOCRISIES
THAT CLEARLY REVEAL
WHO I AM.
WHO I TRULY AM.
LET ME GIVE THEM TO YOU.
GIVE THEM FULLY AND FREE,
IN THE HOPE THAT IN THE GIVING
YOU WILL FINALLY SEE
YOU ARE LOVED.
YOU ARE TRULY LOVED

BY ME.
I OFFER YOU
THE WHOLE OF MY SOUL,
THE FINE AND THE TRUE,
THE MEAN AND THE SMALL.
I WANT YOU TO KNOW THEM,
KNOW THEM COMPLETELY
AND TO KNOW,
IF YOU LOVE, THAT YOU LOVE
BECAUSE OF THEM ALL.
   LAURA.
THAT A MAN MIGHT LOVE ME,
I COULD NEVER BELIEVE.
AND WHENEVER I WAS THREATENED
WITH A HEART ON A SLEEVE,
I WOULD RUN.
I WOULD ALWAYS RUN.
NOW YOU SAY YOU LOVE ME
AND IT TERRIFIES ME.
FOR I UNDERSTAND, AT LAST,
THE ONLY WAY IT CAN BE
IS TO STAY,
IS TO SIMPLY STAY
AND SEE.
I OFFER YOU
THE WHOLE OF MY SOUL

(Exultantly, MICHAEL joins her in counterpoint.)

   BOTH.
THE FINE AND THE TRUE,
THE MEAN AND THE SMALL.
I WANT YOU TO KNOW THEM,
KNOW THEM COMPLETELY,
AND IF THEN WE SHOULD LOVE,
IT WILL SHOW
THAT I LOVE,
YOU WILL KNOW

THAT I LOVE
BECAUSE OF THEM ALL.

(Still unable to touch, THEY move gently, hesitantly, to embrace each other, symbolizing their minds' complete union in an act of telepathy. The LIGHTS fade.)

Scene 5

(The fadeout has left us in darkness. We hear REBECK's voice.)

REBECK. It's still ringing. Nobody's home.
MICHAEL. The police are always home.
REBECK. I should never have agreed to this.
LAURA. We can't let Sandra go to jail for something she didn't do!

(The LIGHTS come up dimly. The scene is the interior of Campos' office. MICHAEL and LAURA are on either side of REBECK, who sits at Campos' desk with a phone to his ear.)

REBECK. It's too dangerous—*(Into the phone.)* What? Now we're on hold!
MICHAEL. Don't worry. Campos always does his rounds now. We have plenty of time.
REBECK. *(Petulantly—HE doesn't want to be here.)* I don't know why you bothered to write a suicide note at all. Not if you were just going to hide it.
MICHAEL. They should have found it by now. I left it in such an obvious place. CRIME AND PUNISHMENT. The leatherette edition.
REBECK. I wish they'd hurry up and—

(HE stops dead in his tracks as the LIGHTS come on full. Standing in the doorway is CAMPOS. HE is swaying slightly and holding an empty bottle of rum. HE walks unsteadily across the office, takes the phone from REBECK and hangs it up. HE begins rummaging in a drawer, forcing REBECK to move aside. HE finds a new bottle of rum, opens it, and takes a large swig. Then HE looks in the general direction of MICHAEL and LAURA.)

CAMPOS. Damn. *(HE takes another swig, then another look. HE rubs his eyes.)* Goddamn!! *(HE turns to REBECK and proffers the bottle.)* Want some?

MICHAEL. Don't panic, Jonathan. We'll think of something.

(Terrified, REBECK takes a drink and chokes.)

CAMPOS. Good stuff, huh? *(HE takes the bottle back, drinks again, looks once more in the direction of MICHAEL and LAURA.)* Don't work too well, though.

MICHAEL. Just get up quietly and leave. He'll never remember. He's drunk.

CAMPOS. Am not drunk!

LAURA. Michael, he heard you.

CAMPOS. 'Course I did. Not drunk.

REBECK. *(Terrified of the answer.)* Who did you hear?

CAMPOS. Them.

REBECK. Them?

CAMPOS. *(Pointing at MICHAEL and LAURA.)* Them.

REBECK. You heard them?

CAMPOS. I said that. *(Another long swig. To MICHAEL and LAURA.)* Didn't I?

(MICHAEL and LAURA nod in amazement.)

CAMPOS. *(Another offer to REBECK.)* The secret's getting drunk. They go away when you're drunk. Want some more?

(REBECK pushes the bottle away.)

MICHAEL. Get him drunk, Jonathan. He'll forget.

CAMPOS. Will not. Can't ever forget. Goddamn ghosts. *(To REBECK.)* Don't know how you stand it. Talking to ghosts all the time. Livin' with 'em. You gotta be crazy. That's what I told the bird. *(Another long drink.)* He's crazy, man.

LAURA. You mean the raven?

CAMPOS. The bird. With the big mouth. I give him stuff sometimes. For him. The crazy guy. You gotta help crazy people. That's what he says. The bird, I mean. *(HE takes yet another drink.)* I didn't tell you that.

REBECK. *(Grabs the bottle away from him in mid-swallow.)* Give me that. *(REBECK guzzles a good one.)* How could he do that? How could he tell?!

CAMPOS. Shhh!

REBECK. He had no right! *(REBECK chugs some more.)*

CAMPOS. Don't blame the bird. I already knew.

REBECK. How?

CAMPOS. You snore. Loud. Ain't never seen no ghost that snored.

REBECK. Why didn't you throw me out?

CAMPOS. I don't mess with crazies.

REBECK. I am *not* crazy!

LAURA. Calm down, Jonathan.

CAMPOS. And I don't mess with ghosts, either.

MICHAEL. And what have you got against ghosts?

CAMPOS. Got nothin' against 'em. Just hate seein' 'em. Ain't right.

REBECK. *(Sloshed.)* It's a gift.

CAMPOS. Horseshit. Hang around a graveyard long enough, anybody can do it. Don't wanna do it. Ain't dead yet. Talk to the dead when I'm dead.

REBECK. If you hate it so much, why don't you quit?

CAMPOS. That's easy for you to say. You got no worries. You got everything you need. Even a fucking flying A&P. I got a wife. And kids. My wife, she's practical. She thinks you're crazy, too.

REBECK. I don't care what your wife thinks.

(CAMPOS reaches for the bottle. REBECK holds it away from him.)

LAURA. Jonathan, I think you've had enough of that.

REBECK. I don't want that man's help. I don't need that man's help. Tell him that. Go on, tell him!

MICHAEL. He heard you, Jonathan.

REBECK. Well, you tell him anyway.

CAMPOS. Bird's gonna be real pissed at me. *(Looks longingly at the bottle.)* Wish I could get pissed.

REBECK. I'm going to bed. I don't think you can see them at all. You just think you can see them. 'Cause you're drunk.

(REBECK stumbles out, bottle in hand. CAMPO watches him go.)

CAMPOS. *(Enviously.)* Now *he's* pissed.

LAURA. Could you make a phone call for us? It's a matter of life and death.

MICHAEL. And it's local.

CAMPOS. Forget it. You're too late.

MICHAEL. *(Suddenly concerned.)* What happened?

CAMPOS. She got off. They found the note last week. Shit, man, don't you read the Post?

(The LIGHTS fade on the office. [Music Cue #20: MUCH MORE ALIVE (Drunken reprise)] REBECK is stumbling back to the mausoleum at dawn.)

REBECK.
TO HELP A SOUL
TO BE WHOLE
IS A GIFT—IT'S RARE.
I WON'T SHARE IT!
I'M MUCH MORE ALIVE.

(And HE collapses on the mausoleum steps.)

Scene 6

(The RAVEN enters. REBECK is passed out on the mausoleum steps, snoring. The RAVEN drops breakfast, in the form of a Dunkin' Donuts bag, on the steps. HE attempts to wake REBECK. After several failures, HE succeeds by crowing like a rooster. REBECK moans. HE is hungover.)

RAVEN. There's coffee in the bag. Donuts, too. *(REBECK gropes for it.)* Should be a good selection. I stole it from the fattest customer I could find. Lots of jellies and cremes.
REBECK. Oh God. *(HE pushes the bag aside and sits nursing the coffee.)*
RAVEN. He already knew.
REBECK. I know.
RAVEN. Made my job a hell of a lot easier.
REBECK. I'm sure.
RAVEN. I'm only one bird, you know.
REBECK. I thought you spoke only to me.
RAVEN. So call me a whore.
REBECK. He talks to *them,* too.

RAVEN. There's never just one of anything in this world. Didn't your momma ever tell you that?

(LAURA and MICHAEL enter. Upset.)

LAURA. Jonathan, stop them.

[Music Cue # 21: DO SOMETHING]

MICHAEL. Calm down, Laura.
LAURA. You've got to stop them.
REBECK. Stop who?
MICHAEL. I'm being transplanted.
REBECK. Transplanted?
LAURA. They're digging him up. Taking him away. To another cemetery.
MICHAEL. It says "Mount Merrill Cemetery" on the side of the truck. Knowing Sandra, it's probably one step above a landfill.
REBECK. I don't understand.
MICHAEL. I was buried in hallowed ground.
RAVEN. He's a Catholic. And a suicide. That's a no-no.
MICHAEL. Sandra must have insisted.
LAURA. We've got to do something.
STOP THEM.
A FEW MORE MINUTES AND THEN
I'LL NEVER SEE HIM AGAIN.
IT CAN'T BE OVER,
YOU'VE GOT TO DO SOMETHING.
YOU CAN'T LET THEM TAKE HIM AWAY.
WE'VE ONLY HAD BARELY A DAY.
GO SEND THEM AWAY.
RIGHT AWAY.
THINK OF SOMETHING CONVINCING TO SAY.
YOU'VE GOT TO DO SOMETHING!
THEY'RE PRACTIC'LLY THROUGH.
THERE'S NOBODY ELSE

SO IT'S GOT TO BE YOU.
DO SOMETHING!
    MICHAEL. What can he do, Laura? Run down the hill shouting "unhand that spectre"? They'd put him away.
    REBECK. I wish there was something I *could* do.
    LAURA. It isn't fair!
    MICHAEL. What's fair? I did this to myself.
    LAURA.
STOP IT!
I THOUGHT THAT YOU WERE THE MAN
WHO'D LAST AS LONG AS HE CAN.
YOU CAN'T GIVE IN NOW!
WE'VE GOT TO DO SOMETHING.
YOU PROMISED ME THAT YOU WOULD STAY.

(To REBECK.)

DON'T SAY THAT THERE ISN'T A WAY.
IF THERE'S NOT A WAY
HE CAN STAY,
WELL, THEN TELL THEM TO TAKE *ME* AWAY!
WE'VE GOT TO DO SOMETHING!

(Back to MICHAEL.)

I'M STAYING WITH YOU!
HE'S GOT TO ARRANGE IT SO I CAN GO, TOO!

(To the world.)

DO SOMETHING!!
    REBECK. You can't leave the place you're buried, Laura. You know that.
    LAURA. Then dig *me* up, too.
    REBECK. I can't do that.
    MICHAEL. Yes you can. If Campos helps.
    LAURA. Of course.

REBECK. He won't want to. He hates ghosts.

MICHAEL. Then he should be happy to get rid of one.

LAURA.
ASK HIM.
TALK TO HIM, JONATHAN.
YOU CAN PERSUADE HIM.

REBECK. How?

MICHAEL.
JUST ASK HIM
AND IF HE GETS DIFFICULT,
GIVE HIM SOME RUM.

LAURA.
TELL HIM
IF HE REFUSES
HE'LL LIVE TO REGRET IT,
'CAUSE I'LL HAUNT HIM
'TIL KINGDOM COME.

REBECK.
WHY NOT?

LAURA.
JONATHAN!

REBECK
THE TWO OF US
SURELY CAN MANAGE.
WHY NOT??

MICHAEL
HURRY, AND FIND HIM
BEFORE THEY GET THROUGH!

REBECK.
WHY NOT!
AFTER ALL, ISN'T MY JOB
HERE TO HELP YOU?
HERE'S A CHANCE I CAN FINALLY
DO SOMETHING.

We'll do it tonight. He can use the cemetery truck truck. We'll leave the headstone just as it is and no one will ever know.

LAURA. I knew there was a way.
RAVEN. Of course, you'll have to go with him. To the other cemetery. Outside.
REBECK. What?
MICHAEL. He's right. Campos won't do it alone.
LAURA. You can come right back.
MICHAEL. *(With surprise and fear.)* Laura?

(And HE is gone. LAURA is frantic.)

LAURA. Michael!! *(To REBECK.)* You've got to do it!
REBECK. I can't!
LAURA. Then why don't you just die? Die, and make it official!

[Music Cue #22: HOW CAN I LEAVE HERE?]

(And SHE disappears in search of MICHAEL.)

RAVEN. Screwed. Like a light bulb.
REBECK.
IF I GO,
THERE'LL BE NO ONE
WHEN A NEW ONE COMES BY.
IF I GO,
THERE'LL BE NO ONE GUIDING,
CHALLENGING, AND PROVIDING
A CHANCE FOR THEM TO QUESTION "WHY?"
IF I GO,
HOW ARE THEY TO KNOW
WHAT THEY'RE FACING IN THE FUTURE?
HOW ARE THEY TO KNOW!?
—AND HOW AM I?
  Forgive me, Laura.
HOW CAN I LEAVE HERE?
IF I COULD LEAVE HERE,
DO YOU REALLY THINK

I WOULD EVER HAVE STAYED?
I NEEDED REASONS
WHY I BELONGED HERE,
BUT ALL THAT WAS TRUE
WAS THAT I WAS AFRAID.
WHERE DO YOU FIND IT?
THE KIND OF COURAGE
FOR MAKING THE CHANGES
YOU KNOW SHOULD BE MADE?
    RAVEN. Don't look at me. I'm just a bird.
    REBECK.
TAKE A STEP OUTSIDE.
YOU CAN MAKE IT THROUGH.

(HE takes a first step on a solo melody line.)

IT CAN'T BE SO HARD TO DO.
YOU HAVE TO LEARN TO RISK THE JOURNEY.
DON'T GET CRAZY WHERE IT GOES.
NO ONE EVER …

(REBECK begins to chuckle. HE searches wildly through his pockets for Klapper's phone number, which HE finally pulls out, by this time laughing uncontrollably. HE waves it in triumph, like a child with a report card.)

REBECK. Gertrude! Gertrude!!!

(And HE runs off in search of a phone. The RAVEN watches him go.)

RAVEN. *(Softly.)* Schmuck.

[Music Cue #23: RAVEN'S FAREWELL]

(Slowly, the RAVEN unfolds his wings. HE takes a last, long look around the cemetery. Then, abruptly, HE

takes off, flying offstage and then back onstage to exit, for the first and only time, over the cemetery wall, cawing louder and louder all the while until HE is gone forever. As the MUSIC diminuendos, a FLASH-LIGHT suddenly shines in the faces of the audience. It is attached to KLAPPER.)

EPILOGUE

(The main gate of Mt. Merrill Cemetery. KLAPPER is alone onstage, haranguing an unseen gatekeeper. SHE is serving as a diversion while REBECK and CAMPOS rebury LAURA's body.)

KLAPPER. What do you care if it's four o'clock in the morning? You're the night watchman, ain't ya? It's your job to take care of customers. My momma's buried in here and I'm staying until I see her and it's none of your business about what. If it's against the rules of the Mount Merrill cemetery, then you just break the rules of the Mount Merrill cemetery. I pay good money to you people. You call this perpetual care?

(REBECK enters during her speech. Now HE steps forward, puts his arm around her, and starts to lead her away.)

REBECK. There you are, my love.
KLAPPER. Tell him I have to see Momma. Tell him.
REBECK. Now, bubelah, he's only following instructions.

(KLAPPER heaves a sigh and stalks away. REBECK speaks to the gatekeeper.)

REBECK. Please excuse my wife. She has trouble sleeping.
KLAPPER. Psst!
REBECK. Good night. *(And HE crosses to KLAPPER.)*
KLAPPER. It's about time. What were you and Campos doing in there, Rebeck, digging for China?

REBECK. I had to do it, Gertrude,—

KLAPPER. Am I complaining? As long as they're happy, I'm happy. We should all be happy. *(Sotto voce.)* Are they around?

REBECK. I haven't seen them.

KLAPPER. Michael? Laura? You can come out now.

REBECK. Sh!! Gertrude!

KLAPPER. Sorry. I just wanted to say, thank you.

CAMPOS. *(Emerges from the shadows carrying a shovel.)* You coming?

REBECK. No, Campos.

CAMPOS. I got some good rum.

REBECK. No thanks.

CAMPOS. Suit yourself. *(HE turns to go.)*

REBECK. Thanks for helping.

CAMPOS. The bird was right, man. You're crazy. *(And HE exits.)*

KLAPPER. Bird?

REBECK. You don't want to know.

[Music Cue #24: FINALE]

(THEY start off together. REBECK is looking around, hoping to catch sight of MICHAEL and LAURA. As the GHOSTS enter, HE stops, as if sensing something.)

KLAPPER. What is it, Rebeck, you see something?

(REBECK looks directly at MICHAEL and LAURA. But HE doesn't see them. HE shakes his head sadly. Then HE turns to KLAPPER and speaks jovially.)

REBECK. I just hope you know how to find the goddamn IRT.

(KLAPPER takes his arm and leads him off. The COUPLES pass through each other. Neither sees the other. REBECK and KLAPPER continue out through the house.)

KLAPPER. *(As THEY go up the aisle.)* Now, Rebeck, about this bird …

(SHE continues to run on about the bird until THEY exit the house. The MUSIC climaxes. CURTAIN.)

[Music Cue #25: CURTAIN CALL]

COSTUME PLOT

LAURA
I-3
Blue striped dress w/collar
White sandal shoes
Blue socks
II-1
Purple sleeveless dress
White hose
Taupe low heels
II-4
Blue striped dress w/collar
White hose
White sandal shoes
II-6
White knit dress
White hose
White character shoes

KLAPPER
Dark blue dress
Blue hat
Black shoes
I-4
Brown houndstooth dress
Brown hat
Apron
II-1
Dark Blue dress
Black shoes
Blue hat
II-2
Purple floral dress
Purple hat
Black shoes
II-3
Black pants

Black and pink floral top
Straw hat
Pink tennis shoes
II-4
Maroon long shirt
Head scarf
Black pants
Mauve sweater

REBECK
I-1
Dark brown suit pants and jacket
Light grey shirt
Dark green tie
Brown sweater vest
Dark blue shoes
Beat up fedora
I-4
White shirt
Slippers
I-5
Dark brown pants
Light grey shirt
Green cardigan sweater
Red tie
II-1
Dark brown pants
Light grey shirt
Green tie
Mauve sweater
II-3
Yellow pants
Yellow plaid jacket
White shirt
Red "wild" tie
II-4
Burgundy robe w/towel
Slippers

I-5
Dark brown pants
White shirt
Red tie
Light green sweater vest

RAVEN
Black sweat pants
Black cowl sweat shirt
Black cut-off sweatpants
Black socks
Black leg warmers
Black sneakers
Fingerless gloves

CAMPOS
Green short sleeve coverall
Brown cap
Mustache

MICHAEL
I-1
Blue jeans
Blue striped oxford shirt
White sneakers
I-4
Brown wool pants
Light blue oxford shirt
Brown knit tie
Large brown sweater
Brown "Connecticut" shoes
II-6
White oxford shirt
White pants
White shoes

Costume Changes

I-1 **Rebeck**: dark brown pants, grey shirt, dark green tie, brown sweater vest: add hat and coat

I-2 **Klapper**: dark blue dress with hat change to: brown dress, hat, apron

I-4 **Rebeck**: dark suit: change to night shirt
Michael: jeans, blue striped oxford shirt: change to brown wool pants, blue shirt, tie, sweat, brown shoes
Rebeck: night shirt: change to costume for I-1.

II-2 **Rebeck**: brown pants, grey shirt, mauve cardigan, green tie: change to: yellow pants, white shirt, yellow plaid jacket, red tie
Klapper: dark blue dress with hat: change to: purple floral dress, hat with fruit
Michael: Brown pants, tie, blue shirt, brown shoes, change to: jeans, blue striped oxford shirt, sneakers
Laura: purple fancy dress, heels, change to: blue striped dress, white sandals

II-3 **Rebeck**: yellow pants, plaid jacket, white shirt, tie, change to: burgundy robe with blue towel
Klapper: floral dress with hat, change to: black pants, black and pink shirt, pink sneakers, straw hat

II-4 **Raven**: sweat shirt and gloves, change to green coveralls, hat, mustache
Rebeck: robe with towel, change to: brown pants, white shirt, red tie, light green sweater vest
Klapper: black and pink top off: add maroon shirt, mauve sweater, scarf

II-5 **Campos**: remove coverall, mustache, hat, add: sweat shirt, gloves

II-6 **Michael**: jeans, blue oxford shirt, sneakers, change to: white shirt, white pants, white shoes
Laura: blue shirt dress, white sandals, change to: white knit dress, white character shoes
Raven: remove sweat shirt, add Campos outfit

PROPS PRESET LIST

<u>ON STAGE</u>

Baloney (rigged above)
Chess set w/ 3 pieces set up
Box of assorted pieces – open
Padded drop box – US of WALL

<u>OFF STAGE LEFT</u>

McDonalds' bag – weighted
Extra phone numbers (on KLAPPER's pink note paper)
Sandwich and bag (weighted)
Cushion (ruffle facing UP)
Morris chess set
Pink thermos
Flashlight, Bagel Nosh bag w/bagel (lying flat in bag)
Extra KLAPPER handkerchief
Walkman w/tape in and phones (in Morris jacket pocket)

<u>OFF STAGE RIGHT</u>

Gravel boxes – one full, one empty
Vacuum cleaner – plugged in
Pallet w/KLAPPER phone table and phone
Empty rum bottle – no cap
Full rum bottle – with cap
Dunkin Donuts bag – w/fake donuts and empty coffee
  cup inside
Shovel
Chewing gum
KLAPPER keys
Hard candy
Door slam unit
Thud bag, squeaky pulley
Back-up phone bell

<u>PERSONALS</u>

KLAPPER's purse w/lipstick, compact. fan, notepad &
  pen
KLAPPER's blue tote w/NY POST, tissues. pink
  thermos, 1 photo album, crochet
KLAPPER's pink & white tote w/NY POST

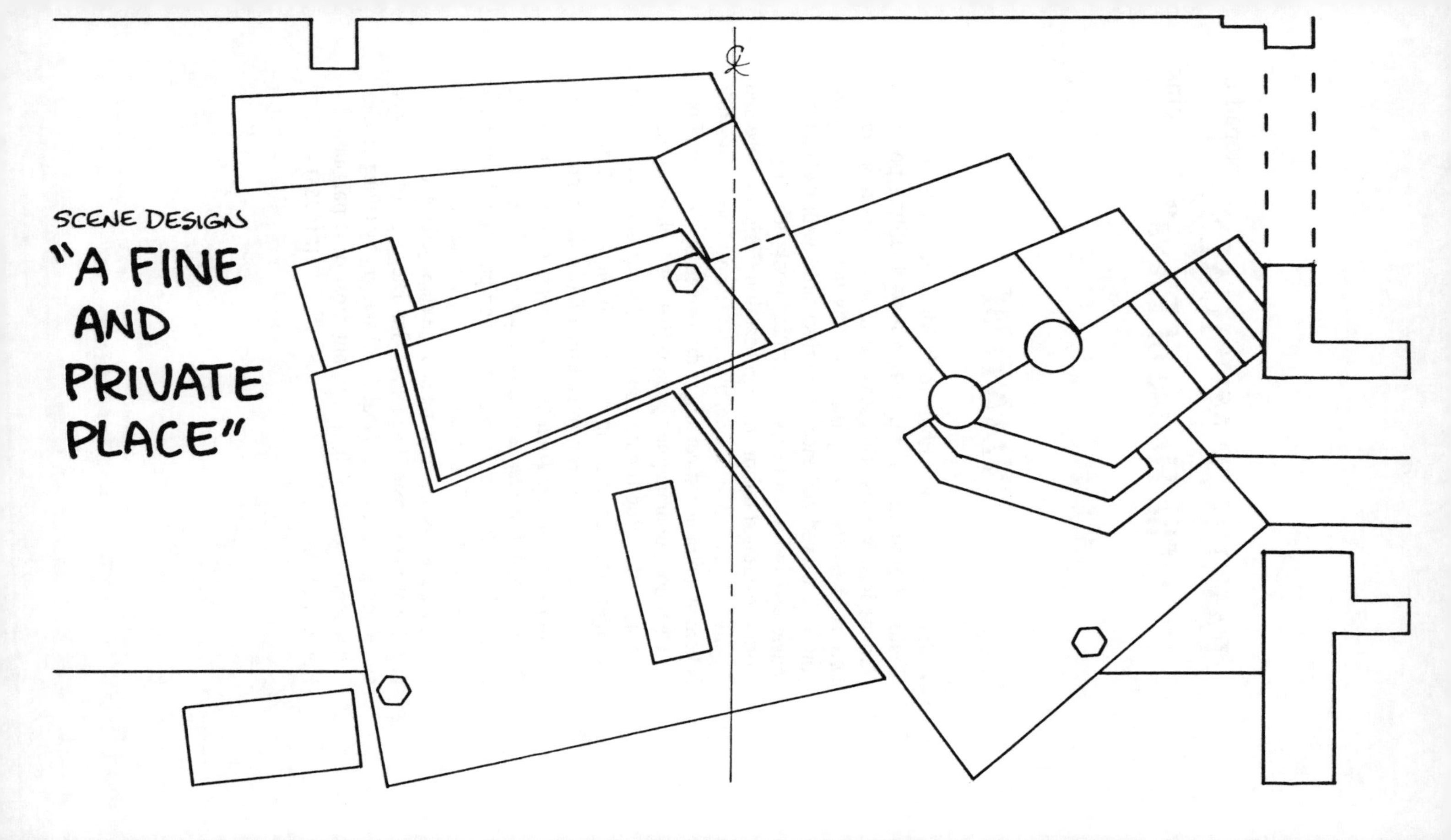

SCENE DESIGN
"A FINE
AND
PRIVATE
PLACE"

FAVORITE MUSICALS *from* "The House of Plays"

PHANTOM

(All Groups) Book by Arthur Kopit. Music & Lyrics by Maury Yeston. Large cast of m. & f. roles—doubling possible. Various Ints. & Exts. This sensational new version of Gaston Leroux' *The Phantom of the Opera* by the team which gave you *Nine* wowed audiences and critics alike with its beautiful music and lyrics, and expertly crafted book, which gives us more background information on beautiful Christine Daee and the mysterious Erik than even the original novel does. Christine is here an untrained street singer discovered by Count Philippe de Chandon, champagne tycoon. Erik, the Phantom of the Opera, is the illegitimate son of a dancer and the opera's manager. He becomes obsessed with the lovely Christine because her voice reminds him of his dead mother's. "Reminiscent of *The Hunchback of Notre Dame, Cyrano de Bergerac* and *The Elephant Man, Phantom*'s love story—and the passionately soaring music it prompts—are deliciously sentimental. Add Erik's father lovingly acknowledging his parenthood as his son is dying and the show jerks enough tears to fill that Paris Opera Lagoon."—San Diego Union. "Yeston and Kopit get us to care about the characters by telling us a lot about them, some of it funny, but most of it poignant."— Houston Chronicle.   **(#18958)**